Don't be afraid of being scared.
To be afraid is a sign of common sense.
Only complete idiots are not afraid of anything.
Carlos Ruiz Zafon

Acknowledgements

First, I want to thank my wife Heather. She has given me more love, patience and understanding than I probably deserve, and for that, I am grateful. Not only has she given me those things, she has also given me a beautiful daughter and son. Heather, I am forever in your debt and I love you with all that I am.

I also want to thank Troy Taylor for pushing me to go the extra distance on this book. When I first found out how long it needed to be, I was hesitant. I didn't think I would be able to do it, but here it is, in all its glory. Thanks, Troy!

I would be remiss to not thank my fellow tour guides, friends and investigators. So thank you Len, Kim, Steve, Sandy, Julie, Pat, and my favorite tour "cabooses," Chas, Matt and my big brother Ben!

Lastly I would like to thank all of those who allowed me to write about their experiences. It means a lot to me to have people share their stories with me. I can't thank you by your real names, but you know who you are!

LIGHTS OUT!

More True Tales of Ghosts from the Lighter Side of Darkness

BY LUKE NALIBORSKI

A Whitechapel Press Publication from Apartment #42 Productions

Original Cover Artwork Designed by
© Copyright 2013 by April Slaughter
Back Cover Additions by Josh Adams

This Book is Published By:

Whitechapel Press
A Division of Apartment #42 Productions
Decatur, Illinois / 1-888-GHOSTLY
Visit us on the internet at
http://www.whitechapelpress.com

First Edition – May 2013
ISBN: 1-892523-81-7

Printed in the United States of America

Table of Contents

INTRODUCTION

Well, here I am, back with version 2.0 of my ghostly adventures. As I write this, it's been five years since my last book came out. It's always been in the back of my mind that I wanted to write another book, but it was difficult to find the time.

Since the last book, my wife Heather and I have added a new addition to our family: my new belly. It seems as though my loafing around and enjoyment of fast food have finally caught up with me. All kidding aside, Heather and I welcomed our true newest addition, a son named Jett, in December 2008. It's not easy to find the time to have adventures and then write about them afterwards while raising a family.

Although the adventures have slowed down, it doesn't mean they've been without substance. Several investigations have uncovered possible ghostly activity. The Alton Hauntings ghost tours have been very active. I've also acquired many new stories from friends and relatives. This book is actually quite a bit different from my first book, *The Lighter Side of Darkness.* In that book, every story was from my own personal experiences. This time, about thirty percent of the stories are from my personal experiences. The rest happened to other people, among them friends and coworkers. This goes to show that you don't have to be a paranormal investigator to have ghostly experiences. In these cases, my witnesses were the ones being sought out by the ghosts.

As I write this, it's October. The Halloween season is here in full force. I am busy as all get out, but it's still nice to be able to take the time to reflect on Halloweens past. I am one of those people who like to reminisce. I grew up in the eighties, one of the greatest decades ever. There was great television, awesome toys, incredible music, and little or no concern about danger when going trick-or-treating!

As with my first book, I'll begin with some of my childhood stories. They will be ghost-related, so it's not like I'm going to talk about fishing trips with my grandpa or school field trips where I brought along my *Dukes of Hazzard* lunchbox. Those were great times, but I'll keep my stories to the subject at hand.

I grew up in Belleville, Illinois, in a house that I believe was haunted. Although I related several experiences that I had while living in the house in my last book, there is another one worth mentioning. Growing up, my brother Sam and I were big fans of Motley Crue. We had heard about how you could hear hidden messages if you played certain records backwards, and we decided to do this one day when my parents weren't home. Sam, one of his friends and I gathered in Sam's basement bedroom and put a Motley Crue album on the turntable. My brother Ben was in his room across the hall. He was busy building a model or something and had no interest in what we were doing. As we began to play the record backwards, we started hearing things in the recording. It was a long time ago and I don't remember exactly what the words were, but I recall them as being very weird. We listened uneasily, playing the record over and over for about fifteen minutes. Then things got strange.

The final time we played the record backwards, one of the cabinet doors in the basement suddenly slammed shut on its own. After that, we decided we were done listening for backwards messages. We thought it would be better – and *safer* -- if we just played the record the usual way. It played normally for a minute or two and then it stopped. To our alarm, it began to spin backwards, and we heard the spooky phrases again. We had hoped to have an unusual experience when we began the experiment, but this was too much. The three of us took off. We ran pell-mell up the stairs, through the kitchen, past the dining room and into the living room. I remember being in the lead at that point. Upon noticing that the front door was open, with the screen door the only obstacle to my escaping the house, I elected to do a spinning mule kick on the unsuspecting screen door. It burst open and out we flew.

Back in his room in the basement, my brother Ben had no idea what was going on. He heard the pandemonium as we fled Sam's room after the record started playing backwards by itself. From the sound of our startled cries and our footsteps thundering wildly up the stairs, he knew something bad must be happening. In a panic, he threw down whatever it was he was working on, and ran up the stairs and out of the house. Once outside, we all felt safer. We didn't go back in the house for several hours. When we did, we avoided going into the basement. Fortunately, my room was on the first floor. That was the first and last time we played a record backwards.

Me with the late Bill Hinzman, one of the zombies from Night of the Living Dead.

I remember one time in particular when I got a very creepy Halloween mask. It wasn't meant to represent any specific character; it was just a terrifying mask, and that was enough for me. It was a man's face, with black curly hair, sunken eyes, wrinkly flesh, and a deranged smile. Now that I think about it, it was kind of a really haggedout version of Tim Curry in *The Rocky Horror Picture Show.* Looking back on it, the mask doesn't seem all that scary, but things look a lot different to the eyes of a child. Believe me, I had some sleepless nights just knowing that mask was in my closet.

In preparation for the Halloween festivities, I decided I would do a test run with the mask to see if it was up to par with my exacting standards in looking absolutely horrific when I went trick-or-treating. My younger cousin, who was five or six at the time, was at our house that evening, and I gleefully anticipated scaring the crap out of her. It was dark out, and I was feeling prankish as I grabbed the mask and headed out the door.

My aunt had parked her car near one of my favorite hiding places where two bushes grew side by side, creating a nice gap between them near the ground. The bushes were thick enough to conceal my hiding spot quite well. I made use of this particular hiding place when my brother's trouble-making friend threw a snowball at a car that was driving by one winter. The enraged driver hit the brakes, jumped out of the car and chased my brother and his friend. I ducked into the bushes and waited until the coast was clear before fleeing to the safety of the house. That story illustrates how useful my hiding spot was.

On the night that I decided to test out my Halloween mask on my little cousin, I put the mask on and crouched in the bushes, waiting for the chance to pounce. About fifteen minutes later, my patience was rewarded as the front door opened. Out came my aunt and my cousin. My mom stood at the door saying goodbye as my targets moved closer. As soon they walked around the side of my aunt's car directly in front of me, I jumped out and screamed like a wild animal caught in some kind of torture device. My cousin started crying and buried her face in my aunt's stomach. My mom started yelling at me. I remember hearing, "What were you thinking, blah, blah, grounded, blah, blah, not going to your friend's house, blah, blah, apologize." There may have been some other things that I missed, but I got the point. Thankfully she let me go trick-or-treating.

I actually did feel bad about frightening my cousin, but more importantly, I knew my mask was going to work out just fine. Look out Halloween, there's a new sheriff in town, and he's scary!

Me with Dee Wallace – One of the great sci-fi/horror movie mothers – *E.T. the Extra-Terrestrial* – *Frighteners* and more!

As I stated before, I grew up in Belleville. Although it was a large city, my brothers and I turned our Halloween trick-or-treating focus elsewhere. My grandparents lived in a wonderful, quiet little town called Smithton, Illinois. It was a perfect place to take candy from a sweet and innocent older population.

We would literally spend hours trick-or-treating. We had it all planned out. There were three of us: my oldest brother Sam, my middle brother Ben, and myself. We had it down to a science. Only four years separated the three of us, but our knowledge of trick-or-treating was amazing. For example, there was one house that always gave away popcorn balls. We would hit it early on. Not because we particularly liked popcorn balls, but because there was a guy in another part of town who would buy popcorn balls from you with a half-dollar coin. He had a huge punchbowl full of fifty-cent pieces by his front door. Do you think you could leave a bowl of money by the door in today's world? That's why I loved the eighties; there seemed to be a lot more trust in those days.

We would make sure to hit one of our other favorite stops about halfway through our battle plan. At this house, they always provided kids with a can of soda. The soda re-energized us with some much-needed sugar to help us push on for another couple of hours. In today's world, you would never get a can of soda as a Halloween treat. It would either be a bottle of water or a juice box full of something healthy, not worth taking a detour for.

Then there was one of the newer subdivisions. This place was cool because people really went all out to decorate their yards. One house had a funeral scene. You had to walk up to the casket and the person lying inside of it would rise up and give you candy. While you were enthralled with the candy exchange, you failed to notice the guy hiding underneath the table that the casket was on. He would grab your ankle, at which point you would try to run, fall down, and then frantically scramble to gather your candy. It didn't matter if he was a monster or not, we worked too hard for that candy to just leave it behind. If the monster was going to get us, so be it. At least we would go down with a mouthful of candy.

There was another house in that same subdivision where they built a maze in their garage that you had to walk through to get your treat. Although I didn't care for the concept of solving mind games to get candy, we played along. It was a really cool setup, and they put a lot of effort into making the kids have fun, but the walls of the maze were made of cardboard and were not very sturdy. What's the fastest way from point A to point B? Straight through the cardboard walls, of course. Although it was flimsy, I still to this day can remember the effort they put into that maze.

Just down the street from that house, there was a place where a guy would be out in the street, chasing after kids with a real chainsaw. I hadn't seen *Texas Chainsaw Massacre* yet, but I knew enough to realize that a bumbling idiot with a chainsaw was something one should run from, and we did just that. Fast. Even though our parents assured us that there wasn't a chain on the chainsaw, it was still terrifying. Yet we always went back, year after year.

By the end of the night, we would have accrued several pounds of candy. We didn't use paper or plastic bags, either. Oh no, bags wouldn't make it through the night. We needed something much stronger to carry our treats. We used the biggest pillowcases we could find. They could carry a lot more weight and take a lot more abuse than your typical bag. That way, when we were in the last home stretch of houses, and my bag of loot was dragging on the ground, I wouldn't find out too late that there was a hole in the bag and my candy was all gone. Who said you can't learn life lessons from Halloween?

Next would be the long-awaited, official division of the candy ceremony. I felt like the general manager of a sports team. Just as some players don't quite have what it takes, some candies don't make the cut. I hated those peanut butter candies that were wrapped in black or orange waxed paper. I don't remember what they were called, and I never cared to find out. As a kid who took his candy very seriously, there is a hierarchy of treats. Peanut Butter Cups were on top, followed by Milky Way, Three Musketeers and Blow Pops. At the bottom were those darn orange and black things, with an honorable mention going to black licorice. Those would either be given to my parents or my brothers. The candy that made the team would then be savored over the course of several months. I wasn't one of those kids that would eat everything they had as quickly as they could; I made it last. It would sit under my bed, in the pillowcase, waiting. Then, when Luke was hungry, Luke would eat. Oh, did he eat! And life was good.

Today, as an adult, I enjoy decorating my yard on Halloween so I can hopefully help kids have the same kind of memories that I do from Halloweens of old. My wife will handle the trick-or-treating duties with our kids because she really enjoys doing that. In exchange, I will take care of the kids who come to our house for their candy needs. I had wanted to take my kids out trick-or-treating when they got old enough to handle the rigors of what it really means to accumulate a serious candy haul, but I have a reputation to uphold at my house. It turns out that my yard is a popular stop for the kids in the neighborhood. I would hate to let them down, so I continue to decorate and hand out treats.

Generally, I build a pirate scene in the front yard. It has a cemetery with deceased pirates coming out of the ground. There's an old ship's wheel complete with a skeleton captain. I also have an old casket that I put in the yard, with a treasure chest next to it filled with candy. I dress up as a pirate and stand in the casket. I run my fog machine into the casket as well. That way, if a kid is working his way to my house, I can stand in the casket, hit the remote to start the fog machine, and have fog fill up the inside of the casket. Then, when kids come up to get their candy I bust out of the casket, with fog completely engulfing me, and shout, "Who's taking me treasure?" Usually the person jumps or runs away while I chortle "har-har!" like a pirate.

This past year was very eventful. A group of three teenage boys came by who thought they were being cool by going out trick-or-treating without wearing costumes. I waited extra long to pounce out of my casket at them.

These three guys were talking about how they should take the entire treasure chest since nobody was there to stop them. They started laughing, and just when it seemed like they were going to go through with it, I jumped out of the casket and aimed my very unrealistic pirate gun at them while brandishing my shiny, fake plastic hook. One of the guys, who in a squatting position, preparing to hoist the heavy treasure chest, screamed an obscenity and fell backwards into the three-foot-high bushes that line the sidewalk. His two buddies started to run and then stopped at the end of the sidewalk and burst out laughing. Once the first guy had crawled out of the bushes, he sat on the sidewalk catching his breath. Then we all shared a moment reflecting on what just happened. We laughed together, talked about how cool it was that I made a high school kid wet himself, and then as we said our goodbyes, I gave them each one of those darn black and orange pieces of candy and sent them on their way.

But you didn't buy this book to hear about my childhood and how it shaped me into the person I am today. So, turn the lights off, climb into bed, cover up, and enjoy some wonderful paranormal encounters.

Oh yeah…Boo!

1. Are Paranormal TV Shows Hurting the Field?

When take part in speaking engagements at various locales, a lot of people ask me if I watch any of the ghost shows on television. To be honest, I watch very few of them. Frankly, I am not a big fan of some of these shows at all. In fact, I'd have to say that they have made it really difficult for some of us to conduct investigations. Well, perhaps saying it's difficult for us to do investigations is a bit misleading. A better way to put it is that they are making it difficult for us to get the opportunity to do investigations.

Several of these shows tend to mislead people as to how investigations are performed. The cast of one show in particular tends to try and provoke spirits into doing things. They'll put themselves in situations to try and re-enact the event that is suspected to be the cause of the haunting. This, to me, is absolutely ridiculous. When I see it, it just leaves a bad taste in my mouth and has me shaking my head in disbelief. First off, they can in no way capture the essence of what the spirit went through in real life that caused them to pass. Secondly, it's disrespectful to even try.

What are spirits? Are they demons? Are they the lost souls of individuals whose lives were cut short? Are they people who just want to stick around and continue to be with their loved ones? Whatever they are, why would anyone disrespect a spirit? If they are indeed demons, I think provoking them is probably the wrong way to go. If they are lost souls, why would you want to harass them in such a way? I would never treat anyone with anything less than respect in life, and I am surely not going to treat them any differently after their passing. Yet some of these television shows use these kinds of tactics to try and get a response from the spirits.

Of course, this type of intimidation led me to some wonderful enjoyment on one occasion. It seems as though one of the "characters" from the show got scared out of his mind and took off running, screaming like a little girl. After congregating with his posse, he then came back to the scene of the crime and started acting tough, yelling at the spirit and challenging him. I could not help but laugh. He reminded me of a wanna-be tough guy at a bar, smacking his chest and jumping around from side to side, all the time praying that the guy he was challenging wouldn't haul off and punch him. I just wonder if he would have gone back to challenge the ghost if his cohorts hadn't accompanied him.

As in most cases, I tend to dwell a bit longer than I should on subjects. This was supposed to be an intro to my next story, but you'll understand the need for calling out shows like this as I get through the story.

I had the opportunity to do an investigation in the historic district of Belleville in 2011. For those of you who read my last book, this would have been a return to an area that was very productive for us. It wasn't the same house, but it was in the same neighborhood. After hearing the stories from the woman who lived in the house, I couldn't wait to get in there.

Beck contacted me via email about doing an investigation. She was a friend of a friend and had found out that I do paranormal investigations. She had been experiencing unexplained phenomena in her house for a long time but never knew who to contact for help. I am in no way, shape or form, capable of ridding a house of ghosts. I make this very clear to people when I talk with them. What I can do is try to find an explanation for what is occurring. If I can't explain it, at least the homeowner will have peace of mind that they aren't crazy.

I love when I open an email and it starts out like this:

Luke, Hi! My name is Beck and I am friends with Bonnie. She told me that you like ghosts? Well I have one (or 2?). I live in downtown Belleville in the historic district. I'm hoping you can help me figure out what's going on here. The ghost(s) are always nice and sometimes a bit playful. What kinds of things would you like to know? Maybe after hearing about our house and what happens here, you'd like to come over and see if you can sense them too. I just don't want to make them mad. They are always nice and I don't want to "rock the boat" ya know?

Looking forward to our conversations, Beck

I was confident that this was going to be the start of a beautiful relationship. We sent emails back and forth for quite awhile, and I gathered a lot of information about her house and its paranormal activity.

Beck's house was built in 1903. The family that built the house lived there for approximately fifteen years. It was Mr. B., his wife and their children. For four of the years they lived there, they shared the house with Mr. B.'s brother and his family. All told, fourteen people were living in the house. Although the house is large, it is no way suited for fourteen people. Such were the times back then. Unlike today, people actually seemed to enjoy the company of family.

Mr. B. worked in a local factory, and his brother worked as a salesman. They were hard workers who got by comfortably. It helped that they grew a lot of their own food.

The layout of the house today is most likely a lot different than it was when it was first built. Today, there are two bedrooms upstairs, along with a bathroom and a closet. When the house was first built, the entire upstairs was probably completely open. The family would have used it as one large bedroom, dormitory-style. Most of the original hardwood floors are still in place throughout the house. Previous owners left traces that are still there. For example, the name Matthew is written inside the bathroom closet. There's a stick figure drawn on one of the doors, as well as marks to keep track of a child's height.

17

In the basement are several rooms, all unfinished. One of the peculiarities in the basement is that one of the rooms has a place on the ceiling where there are about twenty phone lines present. Perhaps the basement was once used as a telephone operator's office.

Now that we have some of the house's history and a brief layout of its design out of the way, it's time to get to some of the ghostly activity that is occurring in Beck's life.

Beck is a devout Christian. She doesn't necessarily feel that ghosts are lost souls, or that they're just sticking around here on Earth because they loved a particular location. She feels that when someone dies, their soul goes to either Heaven or Hell. However, she is open to the possibility that some souls do get trapped here, but only on rare occasions. Beck thinks that these ghosts (or possibly demons) are the devil's helpers, whose goal is to play tricks on us. She believes that they are here to weaken us and tear us apart, not only in our religious beliefs, but also physically, mentally and emotionally.

Beck had her first run-in with the paranormal when she was very young and living in a duplex on the west end of Belleville. She was only five years old when her family had enough and moved out. She was too young to really remember what kind of paranormal activity took place. Her mom later told her that whatever it was would close doors and occasionally move dishes from one side of the counter to the other when no one was home.

After they moved out, her uncle and his wife moved in. They had a very tense relationship that often led to fights. Although the ghost just played harmless pranks before, the fighting seemed to provoke it. It would throw things across the room. It never physically hurt anyone. Perhaps this was its way of telling them to knock it off.

As stated earlier, Beck believes there are one or two ghosts present in her home. The first one looks like an old man. They have also seen the ghost of a child throughout the home. Beck is not sure if they are separate entities or perhaps the same one appearing in different ways.

Beck, her husband and their daughter moved into the home in 2006. Within their first two months there, one of her daughter's friends had an experience in the basement. The girl, whom I will call Jasmine, was about four years old at the time. She and Beck's daughter were playing around the house and out in the yard. At one point, they decided to go into the basement to play for a bit. Beck wasn't sure how long they were down there when Jasmine came up to the kitchen and said, "Miss Beck, who's the man downstairs?"

The little girl described the man as wearing denim overalls, a red shirt and a hat. Beck told her there was no man downstairs. Then she quickly changed the subject.

A month or so later, another one of Beck's daughter's friends had a similar experience. I'll call her Belinda, because I had a crush on Belinda Carlisle when I was younger. The kids were again playing in the basement when Belinda came upstairs and started talking about the old man downstairs. Beck asked what he looked like and the girl described the same man that Jasmine saw. These little girls didn't know each other, and Beck's daughter didn't know what her friends had seen. This was strange, to say the least. As Beck thought about it, she realized that her family might not be alone in their house.

Beck told me about another odd thing that she has repeatedly experienced. She is an avid reader and a stickler for using bookmarks. Often, when she sits down to continue reading a book, she'll find her bookmark has been either removed or moved to another page. Her first thought was that her daughter was responsible. Beck decided to start putting her books up somewhere high where her daughter wouldn't be able to reach. Despite that precaution, the bookmark continued to be moved. She wondered if her husband could be at fault, but it happened even when he out of town.

The book mischief didn't end there. One night, Beck was lying in bed reading with the bedroom lamp on. The lamp was located on her husband's side of the bed. Beck heard him come home and make his way up to the bedroom. He climbed into bed and immediately turned the light off. Beck informed him that she was still reading and the lamp came back on. After reading for about thirty more minutes, Beck told her husband she was done and that he could turn the light off. Just as he was reaching for the light, it turned itself off.

On another occasion while she was reading in bed, Beck said it felt like someone climbed into bed with her. It felt like something heavy was resting on her. It didn't feel like a person, more like an animal. At one point she said it felt like a cat was walking on her leg. Beck and her family didn't own any animals at the time.

The hallway connecting the upstairs bedrooms
(photo by Beck)

On another occasion, Beck had just finished giving her daughter a bath when her husband came home wanting to take a shower. A bit of a mess was left behind from her daughter's bath, and Beck hadn't had a chance to clean it up. A towel was lying on the floor and there was another soaking wet one hanging over the shower doors. Beck's husband remarked, "I love how you leave towels just lying on the floor." At that, the towel that was hanging over the shower door fell down in a heap. Upon inspection, it appeared to have been balled up and flung away from the shower door. Beck was in her bedroom at the time and didn't see it happen, but she heard the sound it made as it fell.

So far, Beck thought all the ghostly events that were happening in her home were caused by the old man. He's not the only spirit present, though. There is another.

A few months prior to Beck contacting me, she and her husband had an experience that was entirely new to them. They were walking upstairs on their way to bed one evening. Beck was in the lead and her husband was following close behind. All of a sudden, Beck's husband saw a child dart across the hallway. It looked like a little boy. The child ran from the bathroom, down the hallway, and into his daughter's bedroom. He asked Beck if she saw something. Beck replied that she hadn't. He crept into their daughter's room and found her fast asleep in bed. Just then, he saw the little boy duck behind a beanbag chair in the corner. He looked behind the chair, but found no one there.

The ghost boy seems to be playful. He tends to play tricks in order to get attention. He'll move things around, play with toys, and just try to get the family's attention. Most of the playful things that happen in the house are attributed to the boy, but he's only been seen once.

Beck and her family eventually got a cat. As sometimes happens, the cat started to take notice of things that humans can't see. Its eyes will move as if it is watching something move around the room. Sometimes, the cat will meow as if it is greeting whatever it is that it sees. It doesn't hiss or act frightened; it seems to be very comfortable with its invisible companion.

So what do you think? Am I crazy? Talk to you soon, Beck :-)

The beanbag chair the ghost child hid behind
(photo by Beck).

At this point in the email, I was salivating. I couldn't wait to get the opportunity to go over to their home and do an investigation. We shot emails back and forth for awhile, trying to agree on a time to do the investigation. Unfortunately, we were having difficulty finding a day that would work for us both. Then I got another email from Beck that made me want to go there even more.

Here's what it said:

Luke, you are going to freak out at what happened today. I had to share this story with you. So today we were not expecting anyone to come over but there was a knock at the door. And of course, the house had to be a mess as usual when unexpected company shows up. I answered the door and it was my mom's best friend since high school, "Tammy." Tammy had a mutual friend of my mom and her from high school with her. This woman's name is Susan. Susan lives in southern IL now, but grew up in my house. She was 6 in 1955, and moved out of the house in 1962.

They were out driving around, seeing places that they hung out in high school. So Susan told Tammy, "I want to show you the house I grew up in" and she took Tammy to my house. Tammy said, "I know who lives there now, do you want to go in and see the house?" Susan said sure and they knocked on the door. So I let them in and showed them around for a while.

During the tour, Susan told me details of what the house looked like when she lived here. We started on the main floor (in the kitchen) then went upstairs and then the basement. When we were in the kitchen, she was telling me about how it looked back then and all the sudden she got this weird look on her face and then she looked at Tammy, almost like she was asking permission to ask me something. Finally after this awkward pause, Susan said, "I feel totally weird asking you this, but Tammy said you were cool about stuff like this…. um….do you ever sense a presence here… like a ghost?" After asking that question she almost looked ashamed and/or embarrassed.

I said, "Yes! You know him too? It is a 'he' right?"

Susan replied, "Yes!"

I told her about the two little girls who both saw and felt him in the basement and before I could describe was he was wearing, she interrupted me and said "Yes, that's where we've seen him too. He wears overalls and a red flannel shirt, right?"

Oh my gosh, I couldn't believe what I was hearing. I got chills and told her "yes!!! Exactly!" Susan said she would always sense him walking up and down the hallway upstairs (where we've heard him also) and in the bathtub and the bathroom closet. I've known him to hang out in the upstairs bathroom closet too! It was so weird! We were finishing each other's sentences! Also I told her that he likes a certain spot in the basement too, but he favors

23

the upstairs. Before I even pointed to the spot in the basement, she pointed to the same spot I was going to show her, and one other spot in the basement. This is soooooo weird!!!!! I have never met this woman before in my life and all the sudden she's in my house, telling me where my ghost hangs out.

I was not scared, more relieved that I am not crazy. I told her how he is never scary, just playful and it goes through spurts where they'll be lots of activity then nothing for a few months. Susan agreed because that's how it was for her too. I told her how he likes to move my bookmark in my books. She said he never did that in her family. Mostly they just heard him walking in the hallway upstairs (very old squeaky floor), and he'd jiggle doorknobs and occasionally open or close a door. We agreed that he hung out in the basement, but in the upstairs was where he made himself known more often.

This was a crazy weird visit! I was seriously expecting Ashton Kutcher to jump out and tell me that I've been Punked! I got the woman's address, and I am going to write to her and ask her about more questions that I've thought of (about the house and the ghost). I'm still in shock that this has happened. Talk to you soon, Beck :-)

Unfortunately, this is where the story takes a turn for the worse. I could tell that Beck was a bit concerned that I would maybe make the spirit angry by doing an investigation. I told her that that's not the way I do things. She was adamant in not wanting to make the activity start to become malevolent. I did everything I could to explain that everything would be fine and that we treat spirits with the upmost respect.

Once we came up with a date to have the investigation, Beck had to cancel due to her daughter getting sick. We rescheduled for another day. As the day approached, I received an email from Beck saying that she had to cancel again. I told her that it wasn't a problem and that she could contact me when she was ready. At this point, I was starting to get concerned that the investigation wasn't going to happen.

After about a month, I contacted Beck to find out if everything was okay. She said it was. I asked her if she was still concerned about making the spirits mad, and she said she was. She didn't want them thinking that I was there to antagonize them or to try and get them to do things by irritating them. She and her family are the ones who have to live with the spirits. They've gotten along, for the most part, so why ruin the relationship that they've maintained through the years?

At this point, there's no date set for an investigation. I'm hoping that maybe in the future, we can make a visit over there some evening. I do, however, respect a homeowner's wishes. If she's not ready for an investigation, I'll wait patiently for a time when she is. When that day comes, I'll be ready to go.

The concerns that Beck has sounds like they were caused by some of the television shows that are out there now, don't they? The portrayal of some of the paranormal investigators who are currently on TV makes it very difficult for those of us who do things the right way. Whether it's investigators who act like cocky, tough guys, or those who think every investigation needs an exorcism, or those who call anything and everything they encounter a ghost without exploring other explanations, they're making it an uphill battle for the rest of us. Especially since what they see on TV is all the general public has to base their opinions of the field on. Hopefully, in time things will get better.

A girl who went on one of the Alton Hauntings tours that I lead during the Halloween season said I should have my own show because I am an awesome storyteller. First off, boy did I pull one over on her! Secondly, I am not sure I would want my own show. Mainly because I'd want to do it right, but the need to generate ratings would force me to do it wrong. With that, I am not looking for a career in television. I don't have the face for TV anyway; I've got a face for the back of a book, especially since the back is usually face-down.

2. Don't You Realize, Marilyn? It's Me.

When most people think about a house being haunted, they assume that it has a dark history. It's also only natural to assume that the house must be old, but that's not always the case. The following story is a perfect example of how a location doesn't necessarily need to be old or to have a tragic history in order for it to be haunted.

Marilyn and Eddie, parents of a friend of mine, moved into a house in a subdivision of Mascoutah, Illinois, in the early 2000s. The subdivision was a newer one that had been built on former farmland. Marilyn and Eddie's house was built in 1995, although the subdivision keeps growing to this day.

The only relevant history that I could find about the house was that a previous owner, an elderly man, passed away while living there. There are a couple of different stories about his death, depending on whom you ask. If you ask the man's family, they will say he passed away in the hospital. If you talk to the neighbors, who supposedly saw the body covered as it was removed from the home, they would say that he died at home. Furthermore, they said it happened in the dining room. Either way, there is a death connected to the home. As far as the land the house was built on, it's been farmland for as long as anyone can recall.

The former homeowner could be the cause of the haunting, or it may be something that relates to the current family living there. When Marilyn was eighteen, she went through the pain of losing two of her brothers, ages 16 and 19, to drowning. Through the years, Marilyn often felt as if they were still around, but was never sure if it really was them in spirit form or just a way that she developed to cope with her loss. People often cope with death by feeling that their loved ones are still somehow with them. However, a number of strange things have happened in her house that Marilyn feels may be caused by her long-deceased younger brother.

Shortly after she and Eddie moved in, odd things began to occur. At first they were small things that were easy to ignore, but they escalated until the activity became difficult to overlook. Marilyn and Eddie could no longer find natural explanations for what was going on. They started to wonder if they might have a ghost. But how could their house be haunted if it wasn't that old? In this case, the home's age didn't matter. It appeared the activity was being caused either by the former owner, or by Marilyn's younger brother.

Some of the strange things that happen in the house occur only once, while others play themselves out over and over again. It seems as though this haunting is both residual and intelligent. By that I mean that in some cases, the ghost appears to be aware that there are living people in the house and may even try and interact with them. This is called an intelligent haunting. Other times, the ghost appears to be oblivious to the home's current residents. These cases are known as residual hauntings.

One of the first things that happened that caused Marilyn to delve into the possibility that her house might be haunted took place while she was doing some spring cleaning. Marilyn was home alone and had just finished vacuuming the living room carpet. As she vacuumed, she moved backwards, until she was out of the living room with the freshly vacuumed carpet in front of her. She left the living room and went to vacuum another room.

When she returned to the living room, she noticed something very strange. On the carpet in front of the love seat was the imprint of a single shoe. The rest of the carpet was untouched. Whatever had left the shoeprint had done so without walking across the room.

There also appears to be ghostly activity centering around three Elvis figurines that Marilyn displays on some shelves. These are the ones where you press a button and Elvis starts to sing. The button to activate the music is small and takes a certain amount of pressure to operate, and yet all three figurines will sometimes play when no one is nearby. Perhaps whatever is causing them to play is an Elvis fan.

One of the most frequent ways the spirit makes its presence felt is by moving a picture frame. Marilyn has pictures of each of her five grandchildren arranged in a semi-circle on a cabinet in the dining room. The picture of one of the grandchildren, whom I'll call Brandon, seems to be the focal point for this activity.

Brandon's picture is the second from the left in the photo arrangement. On average, once a week, the picture will be turned sideways. If Brandon's picture is switched with another grandkid's photo, it won't move. Marilyn and Eddie have tried changing the placement of the photos and switching frames, but it doesn't make a difference. Only Brandon's picture is moved.

Marilyn's daughter Lillian came over to see her parents one day. She knew about Brandon's photo getting moved around, and she asked if it had moved lately. Marilyn told her it hadn't. Lillian then went into the dining room and asked if the spirit could move the photo for her while she was there. Later in the day, the photo had indeed moved, turning itself a good six inches to the left.

The strange thing about the photo moving, as if a photo moving on its own isn't strange enough, is that Brandon is the spitting image of Marilyn's deceased younger brother when he was that age. Maybe this is his way of letting his family know he's still with them. It could explain why Brandon's picture is the only one that gets turned. Who knows? It's a theory, and ninety-nine percent of the paranormal world is based on theories.

A little more evidence as to why this spirit may be targeting Brandon was provided by an experiment done by Marilyn. She set up another group of framed pictures of her grandchildren in another room. The photos were again placed in a semi-circle. Days later, Marilyn noticed that Brandon's photo had begun to move out of alignment with the others. A few days after that, his photo was turned almost completely sideways.

Brandon's picture is the second from the left. This photo was taken the morning after it moved. (photo by Lillian)

All the others were still in their original places. It seems that this would further show a connection between Brandon and the spirit that haunts the home.

Marilyn's sister has also had her share of experiences at the house. Around 2010, she was sitting in the living room watching TV when she saw something that completely floored her. Out of the corner of her eye, she saw something move. When she turned her head to see what it was, a man was standing in the doorway between the kitchen and the living room. She did a double take, and the man was gone. She saw him very clearly and assumed that it was a family member. Upon investigation, she realized it wasn't.

On another of the sister's visits, her dog appeared to have a few encounters with something out of the ordinary. Several times, they would see the dog staring as if it was watching something. Its eyes would follow whatever it was all around the room. The dog would sometimes get up and follow it into other rooms. The people in the house weren't able to see anything, but the dog could.

At one point during the sister's visit, Marilyn's son-in-law heard a noise from the dining room. The dog ran to where the sound came from and started to act very aggressively towards something. It was normally a friendly dog, but it was barking and growling, and showing its teeth towards something in the dining room. After a minute, the dog must have scared off whatever it was because it turned around and pranced back into the living room with its head held high.

That same visit, Marilyn's sister lay down to go to sleep one night. Her dog was resting its head on the blankets beside her. She is not sure how long she was lying there when she felt as if someone sat down at the foot of the bed. She thought it was Marilyn, but when she sat up and looked, there wasn't anyone there. When she lay back down, she noticed her dog was looking toward the foot of the bed and whimpering as if it was frightened by something.

Marilyn has two dogs of her own, and they also pick up on things going on in the house that the family can't see. One of her dogs is blind and deaf, and yet it still seems to know when something out of the ordinary is present. Often times, Marilyn will find the dogs the dogs staring at something she can't see. They'll sometimes stand guard in front of the garage door and bark as if they're trying to alert her to something, but when she goes to look, there's nothing there. The most common place where the dogs seem to pick up sensations of something unusual is in the dining room. That seems to be where most of the unexplained activity occurs. Whether it draws the dogs to it, or whether the dogs are trying to ward it off is unknown. We will probably never know what it is that our pets can see that we can't. And honestly, do we really want to know?

Most of the time, the dogs are the ones who sense something is not right in the house, but occasionally Marilyn has had weird things happen to her. One day, when she was in the kitchen doing the dishes, she heard a male voice behind her. She assumed it was her husband or her son-in-law, but when she turned around, there was no one there. Her dog, the one who is not deaf, also appeared to have heard the voice. The dog was staring intently towards the doorway that leads to the dining room. Marilyn couldn't make out what the voice said, but she says it was clearly a man's voice and it definitely sounded as if it was in the kitchen with her.

Marilyn has heard other voices in the house. One day, when she was not feeling well, she was lying in bed when she began to hear voices. It sounded like a conversation coming from the living room. Her first assumption was that her husband must have left the television on. He was fast asleep, but she woke him up and got him to go into the living room to turn the TV off. This is a ghost book, so of course the voices weren't coming from the television. The living room was dark and empty, and the voices Marilyn heard seconds before were no longer speaking. Thinking about the voices for a moment, she realized that they didn't really sound like they were coming from a television. Just like the man's voice she heard in the kitchen, she was again unable to distinguish what they said.

Marilyn usually finds herself waking up most morning around five a.m., although it takes her a bit longer for her to finally climb out of bed. Around 5:20 one morning, as Marilyn conjured up the strength to welcome the day, she heard her daughter Lillian call to her from the kitchen. She was surprised to hear her daughter's voice that early in the morning, but she figured she must need something. Marilyn climbed out of bed and went into the kitchen. The room was empty. The lights were off, the doors were locked, and there were no signs of anyone having been there. Concerned, Marilyn wrote down what time she had heard the voice. She was worried that something had happened to Lillian to make her call out to her.

Later that day she talked to Lillian on the phone and told her about what had happened. Lillian couldn't explain it. She hadn't particularly been thinking about her mother that morning, and nothing bad had happened to her. She was paranoid for days afterward, thinking that something bad was *going* to happen to her. She was also a little freaked out that the ghost was able to mimick her voice.

Lillian's young son also had an experience in the kitchen. While the family was seated at the kitchen table eating dinner, he began to look off into the distance towards the front foyer. His father spoke to him, but he was completely oblivious. The family turned to see what he was staring at, but they saw nothing. When they asked him what he was doing, he responded with, "Hi Paul!" After that, he was back to normal, eating and chatting with the family.

The family has no idea who Paul is. The answer would have been easy if the old man who previously owned the house had been named Paul, or if Marilyn's brother's name was Paul, but neither was the case. Whoever Paul was, he may have followed Lillian's family home, because shortly after that, her son started saying hello to Paul there, as well. It only lasted a short while, so maybe Paul left. Or maybe the little boy had an imaginary friend named Paul. One can only guess.

One year during the Halloween season, Marilyn had put up some Halloween decorations. In the living room was a motion-activated decoration. In order for it to go off, someone had to pass by it. It was sitting on a shelf, so for it to be activated, whoever passed by would have to be tall. The pets and the grandkids would be too short to set it off. On several occasions, the decoration activated when no one was around. This would happen at times where only one person was home and they weren't in that part of the house. Sometimes it happened at night, when everyone was in bed. Changing the batteries didn't stop it from happening; neither did moving it to another location.

Lillian also had an experience in the living room. She was sitting on the couch watching TV one evening while she was visiting. From where she was seated, she had to look to her right to see the television on an entertainment center that takes up most of one wall. To the left of the entertainment center is a hallway that leads to the bathroom and the bedrooms. As she was watching the television, she saw something move to the left of the entertainment center. It looked like a shapeless white mist, maybe five or six feet tall and a couple of feet wide. She watched it closely as it slowly moved from the dining room, through the living room, and down the hallway towards the guest room.

Lillian's mouth must have dropped open because Marilyn asked her what was wrong. When Lillian told her what she saw, Marilyn just smiled because she has seen it too. She says it's not anything remotely evil-looking, so she doesn't really get frightened by it. It's more the surprise of seeing something inexplicable that makes it so startling. This mist has been spotted numerous times by several people in the home.

Although the mist usually takes an unrecognizable shape, it did have a different appearance during one of its visits. Marilyn had turned left to head down the hallway to the master bedroom when she was stopped in her tracks by a face floating in front of her. Calling it a face may not be quite accurate, as it was shaped like a face but there were no features. It floated there for a few seconds, and then slowly dissipated. After regaining her composure, Marilyn continued towards the bedroom. As she passed through the spot where the shape had hovered seconds before, she felt the temperature drop. She quickly rushed through the cold spot and into the bedroom, where she remained for most of the night.

Marilyn's husband Eddie has only had a few interactions with the spirit(s). He said he has sensed something strange around the house, but he has never seen the mist and he has never heard the voices. The most common activity that he experiences happens when he is working on the computer in the guest bedroom. Several times, he has heard the sound of a door opening or closing coming from the living room. When I was there interviewing them, he said it sounded like the door to the entertainment center. As an experiment, I had him sit in the guest room while someone in the living room closed the door on the entertainment center. Eddie said the sound was identical to the one that he hears when he's working on the computer. My impression is that Eddie is a skeptic. Skeptics tend to either not experience anything paranormal or they write off anything that they do experience as having some unknown but completely reasonable explanation.

Often times, when Marilyn is lying in bed shutting down for the night, she will feel as if she is being watched. She said she doesn't feel frightened by this; it's just a sensation that she sometimes has. The feeling may be caused by her suspicion that there is something living with them in the house. Marilyn said the feeling of being watched happens in all the rooms but it is most prevalent at night when she's in bed. Perhaps it's because when you're lying in bed in your PJs, you're more vulnerable than you are when you're upright and fully dressed. Think about that as you lie in bed reading this book. If that doesn't make you think twice about sleeping peacefully, you are braver than most.

Sometimes when Marilyn feels like she's being watched, she will feel the mattress shift, as if something sat down on the bed with her. The bed will even show an imprint as if a person actually did sit down on it. I asked her if she ever felt like something touched her while she was lying in bed and she said yes. She said sometimes, when she is alone in bed, it feels as if someone is lying next to her. Of course, I had to ask her if it was a spooning kind of thing, or if it was just a barely-touching-arms kind of sensation. She just smiled, so we'll go with spooning.

Marilyn once had a very vivid dream where she was talking to her grandson, Brandon. Marilyn said to him, "You don't look like your mom or your father, so where did you come from?" At that, her deceased younger brother appeared in front of her, looking the way he did when he was alive. He said, "Don't you realize, Marilyn? It's me." Marilyn felt relieved. She began to feel that the spirit in her home wasn't trying to frighten them; it was just her brother spending time with his loved ones. This made it a lot easier for her to cope with what was going on.

Could Brandon really be a reincarnation of Marilyn's brother? Did he tell her "it's me" to let her know he's the one haunting the house, or because he wanted her to know that he was reborn as Brandon?

Unfortunately, Marilyn's dream may have been a trick by something mischievous and sinister. Perhaps the spirit that visited Marilyn in her dream was the same one that pretended to be Lillian by imitating her voice. Only this time, it was hitting Marilyn in a much more emotional way by pretending to be her deceased brother. Not that pretending to be her daughter isn't bothersome, but I feel pretending to be a lost loved one is a horrible thing to do.

You can judge for yourself, but here's what makes me suspect the spirit may not be who Marilyn thinks it is:

One day, Marilyn was watching Brandon for the afternoon. It was shortly after lunch and they decided to take a nap in the master bedroom. They both dozed off very quickly. After an hour or so, Marilyn was abruptly awakened by the sound of voices.

The voices were coming from the bedroom, but the television was off and the rest of the house was quiet. The voices seemed to be engulfing the entire room, coming from every direction and resonating in her ears. Brandon was still asleep. The voices kept saying the same thing over and over: "Get out!" "Get out!" "GET OUT!" According to Marilyn, it was a chorus of voices, men, women and children, all of them repeating the same words. Marilyn was very frightened. She had heard voices before, but never like this; these sounded threatening. I don't feel Marilyn's brother would frighten her like that. Of course, one could argue that maybe something was wrong and not only her brother, but all the spirits in her life were telling her to get out. Were the voices threatening, or were they protecting? I think in this case, the voices were threatening. I don't think they were caused by her brother or any of her other lost loved ones. However, I do feel that what happened next *was* caused by her brother.

As Marilyn lay there, listening to the chorus of voices and becoming more and more frightened, she was unable to move. After what seemed like minutes of hearing "get out!" ringing in her ears, something put a stop to it. A loud and heavy bang hit the mattress. It made the entire bed shake. At that, the voices immediately stopped. Something or someone had finally had enough and had stepped in and put a stop to the madness. I think it was Marilyn's brother coming to her rescue by warding off the other spirits.

So in my unprofessional opinion, here's what I think about the haunting so far: I believe there are at least two spirits in this house, maybe three. There may be a residual haunting by the previous homeowner. I think he is the misty shape that moves around the dining room, living room, and hallway. I think Marilyn's brother is also there. He watches over the family, moves Brandon's picture around, and just tries to calm things down. I also think there's something else in the house, something darker. This is the source of the voices and whatever is frightening the dogs.

I'm hoping to do an investigation of the house soon. There seems to be a lot going on. I love this story because it illustrates how a house doesn't have to be old to have paranormal activity. Whether a house is already active or the new tenants brought something with them, every house can carry a secret or two.

UPDATE:

I asked my friend to go over to the house a few times one week and take photos of the collection of grandchildren's pictures. I wanted to see whether the frame containing Brandon's picture was moving, and if so, how quickly. After the frame hadn't moved for the first few days, my friend called out to the spirit, "If you want to be in Luke's book, you gotta step it up." The next morning, when she went back to take a picture, this is what she found:

This is the photo she took the morning she told the spirit to do something.

This is the one she took the following morning.

Spooky!!

3. No Free-Floating, Full-Torso, Vaporous Apparition

Libraries have always had an eerie feeling to them, in my opinion. Perhaps it's the dusty smell, the darkened aisles, or just their overall quietness that gives them a ghostly feel. It may be the role that libraries have played in some scary movies that have helped lend creepiness to them. Personally, I think the movie *Ghostbusters* had a lot do with it. I was only seven years old when I first saw it, and that librarian specter haunted my dreams for weeks! There are plenty of libraries across the country that claim to have real spirits, as well. The most famous, in my opinion, being the Willard Library in Evansville, Indiana, where a ghostly Lady in Grey has been seen since the late 1930s.

I heard stories during my time in Mascoutah that the local library was haunted. I had been there several times through the years, but I never experienced anything out of the ordinary. However, just because nothing happened to me does not mean that the library isn't haunted; the ghost just didn't make itself known during the times when I was there.

I spoke at the library a couple of years back, and after I finished, one of the librarians mentioned that the library had a ghost. That intrigued me, and although I wanted very badly to learn more, it wasn't meant to be that night. I had already run over my allotted time and the library was about to close. Fast forward to today, and here I am writing about the ghost after finally getting the opportunity to hear some of the stories.

The first library opened in Mascoutah in 1929. It was run by the Mascoutah Woman's Club and started out with a small collection of books. Through the years, the library continued to grow until it was one of the best in the county. It changed locations several times from its first location on Main Street, into the new City Hall building for a time, and finally to its current home on Church Street.

Through the years, employees and patrons have reported having had unusual experiences in the library. I am sure there are more people who are keeping quiet about their experiences. Sometimes people tend to keep things like this to themselves, especially people living in small communities. Everyone knows everybody, and they don't want anyone to think they are crazy.

Mascoutah Public Library

Before we get to the ghostly tales, we'll start with a brief description of the building's layout. When you first walk in, there is a large room with shelves full of books on both sides. Straight ahead is the check-out counter and office area. The genealogy room is to the left, as well as a couple of other rooms. The children's library and recreational area is to the right. There are several other rooms that can be entered to the right of the main counter area.

One of the employees who worked there in the late 1990s told me about several experiences that she had. To protect her anonymity, we'll call her Alice. For you trivia fans, that's the name of the librarian in *Ghostbusters* who encountered a ghost while working in the stacks of main branch of the New York City Public Library. Alice told me about several things that happened to her as well as to another library employee whom we'll call Ruth, after the actress who played the library ghost in *Ghostbusters*.

Several times at night, when Alice would be working late, she'd hear someone calling her name. These were times when she was the only staff person in the building. Since there were no other employees working at that time, she assumed that a library patron was trying to get her attention. She would look around, but she was never able to find who was calling her, no matter how hard she tried to find the source of the voice. It sounded female, but it was hard to tell because it spoke in a whisper. It would whisper her name a few times and then stop. It seemed to want to get her attention, not frighten her.

Having your name whispered by someone you can't see is something that is difficult to just ignore. Alice said she felt goose bumps rise and her hair stand up every time she heard the voice. When she mentioned the incidents to Ruth, she discovered that Ruth had experienced the same thing, but had kept it to herself. Ruth felt better that she wasn't the only one hearing the whispering voice. Although it still felt spooky, at least she knew she wasn't crazy.

Alice told me she thought a cabinet in the genealogy room is a source of paranormal activity. The cabinet houses lots of large, old books that library patrons use to research their family histories. The cabinet had always been in the same place, but on one occasion it was moved to a different area. Shortly after that, strange phenomena began to occur. It was as if the ghost was trying to let everyone know that the cabinet would be better suited in its previous location.

Alice recalled a time when she was working late one evening. She had been walking up and down the aisles returning books to the shelves. She was standing in front of a bookshelf, holding several books, when she reached up to shelve one of the books. At that, a couple of books flew off the shelf in front of her, nearly hitting her in the face. This frightened her, and she decided the books could wait to be returned to their proper places. That was one of the only times the library ghost seemed malevolent. Alice was shaken up, but she insists that the spirit was just trying to get her attention.

Ruth had a few unusual experiences of her own in the library, besides hearing the whispers. One evening while working late, she heard footsteps walking down an aisle ahead of her. The library was closed and Ruth was the only one in the building at the time. Each time she would catch up to where the footsteps seemed to be coming from, the sound would stop and then start up in a completely different location. No matter how hard she tried, she could never catch up to what was making the noises. Ruth called her husband and had him come over because she thought someone had gotten in somehow. Upon further investigation, the building was found to be empty.

Ruth even experienced being touched by something invisible during one of her nightly shifts. While standing in front of a bookshelf, she felt her necklace start to move on the back of her neck. It felt like someone was fumbling with the clasp. She could even feel her hair moving, as if someone was brushing it aside in order to undo the clasp. It only lasted a few seconds, but it seemed a lot longer. When Ruth turned around, there was nobody there. To her relief, her necklace was still on.

During a Haunted Library event one Halloween, several unexpected things happened to a group of children. There were scary movies and ghost stories. There were even some experiments to try and conjure up ghostly activity. One of the experiments involved placing a bell in the center of a table. The participants would stand around the table and hold hands. Each person was asked to concentrate and silently request any spirit that might be present to ring the bell. With several different groups, the bell did indeed ring, even though it never left the table.

Another group tried the experiment, this time with a different twist. Instead of placing a bell in the center of the table, they drew a circle out of salt. Again, the kids held hands and silently asked the spirit to come forward. At first, it seemed like nothing happened, but as they looked down at the table, they saw that part of the salt circle had been wiped away. It was as if someone had reached out and swept some of the salt away. Nobody confessed to having done it. But just like with my tours, there's always that one person who sabotages the experience to try and scare the others. Sometimes what appears to be supernatural activity is just some idiot wanting attention. Other times, well, you just never know!

Although cold spots are found all over the library, they are most often felt in the children's area. Whatever is haunting the building seems to fancy that room more than any other. Perhaps the spirit is a previous librarian who was fond of reading to the children. I mentioned this theory to Alice, who agreed it was possible. As with most hauntings, we may never know for sure.

One evening, Ruth was busy working when she suddenly felt as if she was surrounded by intense cold. Exasperated, she yelled out, "I don't have time for this! If you are here, go to the light and move on!" After that encounter, Ruth said that the library has been quiet. Well, it's always quiet since it's a library, but I'm talking quiet on the haunting front. Perhaps the spirit has finally moved on. Or perhaps it just didn't make itself known to Ruth any longer because its feelings were hurt that she yelled at her.

After hearing the stories about the strange occurrences in the library, I am not sure what to think. There have been no sightings, no free-floating, full-torso, vaporous apparition as encountered in *Ghostbusters*. There have been possible orb photos taken in the library, but the "orbs" could just be dust from all the old books. It also seems like things occur more often when people are alone in the library, so there have been no multiple witnesses. Hopefully, with the publication of these stories, other people will come forward with their own experiences at the Mascoutah library, and I can be proved wrong by discovering that there were indeed multiple witnesses to some of the events.

I can't say for sure the library is haunted, but the setting is right. Quite often, there have been reports of the ghosts of librarians coming back to the places they loved so much in life. That could be the case here. Or maybe, one of the books in the library has a spirit attached to it. If I could only find out which book, it would be neat to try and find out if the spirit goes along when the book gets checked out. That's something to think about the next time you borrow a book from the library.

4. Free: Furniture With Spirits Attached?

Can ghosts become attached to a personal belonging and travel with that item to new destinations? I believe the answer to this question is a resounding yes! I've heard plenty of stories in my paranormal career that suggest that this can and does happen. Whether it's an old clock purchased from an antique store, a family heirloom passed down from generation to generation, or an item that was purchased on eBay, all of these things have a past. Perhaps someone loved the item so much that they don't want to leave it. Maybe it's a family member who uses the item as a means of staying in touch after they passed on from this world. Whatever the reason, I believe it to be true, and here's a story that plays into this idea perfectly:

I was contacted by a friend of a friend named Andrea who was experiencing some unusual activity at her house that started rather suddenly. Like Beck, whose story I related earlier, Andrea lives in Belleville's historic district, in a house that was built in 1856. She and her family moved in a little over four years ago. Minor things happened almost from the start, like doors slamming shut suddenly and odd noises, but these could have been caused by the wind, or by the old house settling. These things didn't happen often, so when the activity started to escalate, Andrea and her husband, Shane, realized something not normal must be causing it. They began to suspect that some furniture they had recently acquired might have a spirit attached to it.

In September of 2012 Andrea's mother-in-law passed away. Andrea and Shane were faced with the task of cleaning out her home. They decided to keep some of the mother-in-law's belongings, rather than sell them off at an auction or an estate sale. Among these were some basic household wares as well as some beautiful old furniture and family heirlooms. Having his mother's things around him would be a comfort to Shane, and what better place to display antiques than in their antique home? They packed the articles up and brought them home.

The first incident that made them realize something strange was going on in their home happened one morning about three weeks later. Shane called Andrea at work to ask if she had left the desk light on in the computer room. He had discovered the light was on as he was getting dressed for work. His initial thought was that Andrea had left it turned on the night before and he just hadn't noticed it, but he had walked past the computer room on his way to the bathroom, and he didn't recall the light being on then. Andrea told him she hadn't been in the computer room for a few days so it couldn't have been her. Shane turned the light off and headed off to work.

When Andrea got home later that day, she made her way to the computer room to pay some bills. As she tackled bill after bill, she realized that something was not right. Something about the desk seemed different. It took a few moments before it finally hit her that the desk lamp was missing. She thought Shane must have moved it after finding it had been left on earlier that morning. She continued paying bills. Then, something caused her to turn around.

The last time Andrea went shopping, she had purchased some cases of soda. These were placed on the floor in the computer room to get them out of the way. When she turned around in her office chair, she noticed the desk lamp was sitting inside one of the opened cases of soda. Puzzled, she phoned Shane and asked him why he had put it there. Shane denied doing it. He said he had turned the lamp off and left it on the desk as usual before leaving for work.

After discussing the event further, Shane had a strange feeling that his deceased mother was responsible for the lamp activity. Maybe by turning on the light, she was letting him know that she was still there with him.

The cases of soda were Pepsi, which just so happened to be his mom's soda of choice.

After this event, Andrea hoped things would return to normal, but that wasn't to be. Having returned home from work one evening, she did the dishes and then sat down on the couch to start her homework for a class she was taking. She didn't get very far into her studies when she noticed her three dogs were staring into the kitchen. They would stare a bit and then start whining as if something was frightening them. Andrea ignored them until the sound of something falling to the floor in the kitchen made her jump. She got up from the couch and went to have a look. On the kitchen floor were several pieces of silverware that she had just washed. Andrea found this odd because she had deliberately placed the silverware away from the edge of the counter, where it was not likely to fall off. From where it lay scattered, it looked as if it had been thrown.

The hutch that had belonged to Andrea's mother-in-law
(photo by Andrea

The activity in the house happens most frequently in the kitchen. Andrea wonders if it's because an antique hutch that belonged to her mother-in-law now resides in the kitchen. Frequently, around six or seven o'clock at night, her dogs will sit in the kitchen doorway and bark at absolutely nothing. Well, nothing that Andrea or Shane can see. I asked Andrea if her mother-in-law and the dogs got along well and she said they did. Andrea's mother-in-law was an animal lover who lavished attention on the dogs when she came to visit. She may still like dropping by to visit the dogs. As far as why her spirit seems to prefer to hang out in the kitchen, we don't need to look any further than the hutch, in my opinion. Maybe she was so attached to the hutch that she came with it. Or maybe she came to the house first and found herself drawn to the kitchen because her hutch is there now.

Andrea and Shane have a lot of items adorning the walls of the kitchen. Some hang from nails, others are displayed on shelves. Sometimes at night, Andrea said she hears the sound of something crashing coming from the kitchen. She or Shane will run downstairs and find several of the wall decorations lying scattered on the floor. Sometimes they won't hear anything in the night, but when they come down for breakfast, items from the walls will be on the floor.

One of the main things in the kitchen that attracts the spirit's attention is a family heirloom, a clock that formerly belonged to Shane's mother. On a handful of occasions, this clock has been found lying on the floor as if it simply fell off the wall. Other times, it will be found somewhere in the house. Neither Andrea nor Shane has ever relocated it, and yet the clock seems to move from its place on the wall with no help from anyone. At least, with no help from anyone of this world.

Strange sounds seem to be happening inside this home. A lot of the noises could be caused by the house being almost 160 years old, but perhaps not all of them. Andrea's mother-in-law used to walk with a cane. Often times, Andrea will hear a tapping or clicking noise that

47

sounds a lot like the sound her mother-in-law's cane made.

The clock (Photo by Andrea)

Upon investigating the source of these noises, nothing is ever found. Another sound that frequently occurs is that of silverware clinking. It sounds like someone is setting a table, or perhaps putting silverware away in a drawer. These noises have been loud enough to wake Andrea up in the middle of the night. When she goes to the kitchen to check, nothing will be out of place.

Quite often, when Andrea is in the living room studying or watching television, she will hear the sound of someone walking upstairs. Usually these sounds are accompanied by a clicking noise. The sounds will work their way from one end of the upstairs floor to the other. It might not necessarily be Andrea's deceased mother-in-law. We always have to rule out other possible causes. It could be the house settling, or water pipes expanding and contracting, or hundreds of other possibilities.

Other activity that happens in the home involves the back porch door. The door tends to open and slam shut on its own. It doesn't happen often, but when it does, the sound can be heard all over the house. This has only occurred since the death of Andrea's mother-in-law.

Andrea also mentioned that one of the shelves in the living room seems to be a focal point for ghostly activity. There are various items displayed on the shelf. Sometimes when Andrea gets up in the morning or comes home from work, all the shelf's contents will be strewn about the living room. Nothing is ever broken. The items seem to always be placed with great care.

Andrea suspects that the sound of footsteps moving upstairs might have something to do with an old record player that was another one of her mother-in-law's favorite possessions. She owned it almost her entire life, which is why Andrea and Shane wanted to take it: to make sure it went somewhere where it would be loved the same way she had loved it. Andrea wonders if it is because of this record player that she hears the sounds of footsteps. Could her mother-in-law be checking on her treasured possession to make sure it's being cared for properly? Or could her spirit be dancing to music that only it can hear?

With the exception of a few things I mentioned at the beginning of the story, most of the activity in this home began after Shane's mother passed away. Andrea and Shane are not scared in the least, and have even welcomed these occurrences. Are the items that they brought into their home the cause of the activity? Is Andrea's mother-in-law's spirit trapped in one of them? Or is her spirit simply attached to the things that she loved so much in life? I think she is just watching over things and letting her family know she is there.

5. Trouble Sleeping? Try Bedding Down With a Ghost!

Back in 2010, I had the opportunity to speak at the Mascoutah Public Library. I love telling stories. It doesn't matter how many people show up. As long as there is one person who is listening, I'll keep talking.

One of the main reasons I was excited about speaking there is I was hoping to get some leads for possible investigations. Mascoutah is my hometown. It would be nice to be able to do an investigation in my own backyard rather than having to drive all over the place late at night.

A woman named Laura attended my presentation and came up to me after the event. Since it's my story, I'm going to go ahead and say it was the best presentation she had ever been to. She told me about a ghost in her house that has been there as long as she can remember. She was hoping that maybe I could come over and do an investigation. I was very excited to do so.

We traded emails back and forth, and I was able to learn a lot about the home prior to visiting it. I always like to get an idea of what I am getting into prior to checking out a location. Since this house was only a few blocks from mine, it was easy to find the time to go there. In fact, I drive past the house all the time. I've always really liked the way it looks. It had a vibe to it that made me think it could possibly be haunted.

The house was built in 1858 and is located on the west end of town. Laura said she was pretty sure it used to be a popular place for a local club to hang out. She had heard that they used to have dances there. The house isn't very large, so I would have to think the dances weren't very extravagant. The front yard is fairly small as well, and there are some beautiful old cobblestones in the back yard.

Laura's family moved into the home in 1967. Both of her grandparents passed away there, but Laura and her family didn't feel that they are the spirits that are present. The main spirit is thought to be that of a man. They called him George, not for any particular reason, just to give him an identity.

Laura experienced paranormal activity in the home for the first time almost twenty-five years ago, when she was eleven years old. It was her uncle's house at the time. Laura wasn't feeling very well early one evening and decided to lie down on the living room couch. She was having trouble going to sleep, so her uncle told her to go upstairs to his room, where she would be more comfortable. Laura did as he suggested and bedded down and closed her eyes. The next thing she knew, she could feel someone or something lying down in bed beside her. Whatever it was, it was heavy enough to make the mattress move. When she opened her eyes, there was nothing there.

Laura wasn't sure how she could tell, but she said it seemed like whatever was there was facing her the entire time. She couldn't shake the feeling of being watched, even though she couldn't see anyone.

Laura said she didn't feel threatened or scared. She closed her eyes again and fell asleep for a solid two hours. When she went back downstairs, her uncle and grandmother looked at each other with mischievous smiles and made a comment about her having a good nap. Laura was wondering what was going on when her uncle asked if she noticed anything weird while she was upstairs. Laura began to describe the feeling she had of someone lying in bed with her. All the while, her grandmother and uncle's smiles grew bigger. They told her there was a ghost haunting the upstairs bedroom, one that only comes around when there's a lone female present.

51

To me, that seems like it would scare the heck out of an eleven-year-old girl. Not Laura, though. She took many more naps in the upstairs room. As long as she was alone, the ghost, whom they took to calling George, would usually show up. He always slept on the right side of the bed and he never did anything to scare her. In fact, Laura said she always slept very soundly in that room. She didn't even have to be tired; all she had to do is lie down and she was out.

Years ago, Laura's mother slept in the room and had the same experience of the ghost making itself comfortable in the bed. Laura's aunt also experienced sharing the bed with George, but she didn't take it quite as well as Laura and her mother. She was so frightened that she moved to another room and refused to sleep in the attic bedroom ever again. Even though the spirit never did anything to harm anyone, having the sensation of an invisible person in bed with you would be very alarming to most people.

The bed frequented by the spirit of George

As Laura stated, if a man is present, the ghost wouldn't come around. Her uncle had never been visited, even though it was his room that the ghost frequents.

Neither have any other men who stayed overnight in the room through the years.

Laura talked about another spirit in the house, one that hangs out on the first floor. She said she couldn't really tell what it is for sure. Sometimes it seemed like it could be human, sometimes she felt as if it was a cat. Usually, her cats experienced it before anyone else did. The cats would be fine one moment and the next they'd start running around and hissing at something that wasn't there. Sometimes they'd be calm and just start meowing at something, other times they were visibly frightened.

After reviewing the information Laura sent me about the haunting, I set up a time to go out to the house for an investigation. I wanted very badly to bring a female investigator with me, not for a woman's opinion or anything; I wanted her for bait. If the spirit upstairs only comes out for the ladies, then I needed a lady. Unfortunately, the best I could do was my friend Matt, who's far from feminine. But since I don't do investigations alone, I was happy with whomever I could get.

We showed up on the appointed evening and came in through the back door. When you first walk in, you come into a screened-in porch. Then you go through the laundry room and into the kitchen. Laura took us straight upstairs into the attic. It was once one big room, but it had been divided into two areas, one of which was made into a bedroom. Walking through the door to this room it like walking through a time portal. There's wood paneling on the walls and several black light posters. There was even a Farrah Fawcett poster. It was like stepping back into the '70s. My father-in-law went to school with Laura's uncle, and when I told him I was doing an investigation there, he said he didn't think that room had changed since he was there in high school.

Laura showed us around a bit, and pointed out some of the hotspots for activity. Obviously, the bed in the attic was going to be a focal point for the investigation. I set my EMF detector there. The idea behind EMF detectors is that they are able to pick up spirit activity by indicating changes in electromagnetic energy. When a spirit is present, the needle on the detector will begin to spike. It's important to make sure the detector isn't picking up on man-made electrical sources before you consider your finds to be paranormal.

I set up my video camera on top of the entertainment center, next to an assortment of VHS and cassette tapes. Yep, VHS and cassette tapes. I told you nothing had changed in that room for decades! I aimed the video camera at the bed. If there was any kind of movement, the camera would pick it up. If the EMF detector spiked, the camera would not only pick up the needle spiking, but also the god-awful sound it makes when it gets set off.

After setting up the equipment, I spent a few more minutes admiring the lovely Farrah Fawcett poster, and then we made our way back downstairs. The upstairs bedroom would be a controlled area that was off-limits to everyone except George, if he cared to make an appearance.

We sat down at the dining room table and Laura told us some more stories about the house. She said sometimes when they go upstairs, they experience what they call warm spots. Now, if you are reading this, you most likely have an interest in ghosts. In that case, I am sure you've heard of cold spots. For those of you who do not know what cold spots are, I'll break it down for you: Cold spots are basically thought of as a way to know if a spirit is present. Spirits are believed to need energy in order to manifest. Heat is a form of energy. If a spirit is trying to make itself known, it may draw the heat out of an area as a means of acquiring energy. That heat-drained spot becomes a cold spot. What makes cold spots unique is that you can put your hand into one and feel the cold. Imagine yourself sticking your hand in a freezer, and then pulling it out. It goes from cold to warm. It's the same with cold spots. You can literally stick your hand into them, feel the cold, and then pull your hand back out and it feels warm again. This can be repeated until the cold spot either moves somewhere else or dissipates entirely.

The creepy stairs leading to the upstairs bedroom

So, what about warm spots? Is it getting so scared that you feel a warm trickle running down your pants leg? Is it perhaps a spirit that has gathered sufficient energy and is projecting warmth? I was baffled by this, primarily because I have never experienced this type of activity. I asked Laura if a heating vent could be producing these warm spots. She said it wasn't possible because they can be felt in different locations, and at times of the year when the heat is turned off. I really am not sure what to think about this. Maybe on some investigation down the road I'll get to experience a warm spot and then I can find out the cause first-hand.

Another spirit that may haunt the house is that of a former pet. Laura's family used to have a very playful cat that was notorious for getting extra rambunctious around the holidays. Its favorite pastime was climbing around in the Christmas tree. The first Christmas following the cat's death, the family would notice the tree shaking as if the cat was still climbing around in its branches. The tree would shake and ornaments would fall. When they would check to see what was causing it, they would find nothing. They thought they knew who was visiting, and were not scared in the least.

After Laura finished telling me more stories, I decided it was time to do an experiment. If George only comes out when there is a woman present, then why not have a woman in the room? So that meant Laura was the odd girl out. She was going to have to take one for the team and go up to the room by herself. I told her to go upstairs for about twenty minutes and then come back down to the dining room. Matt and I would sit in the kitchen and wait.

Laura agreed and off she went. Matt and I talked for a bit and checked the Cardinals score on his phone periodically. Twenty minutes passed quickly, but Laura didn't come back downstairs. I figured we'd just wait a bit longer and then go and retrieve her.

Thirty minutes passed, and Laura and still hadn't come back downstairs. I was getting kind of excited at this point. I figured the reason she hadn't returned was because she was experiencing all sorts of activity up in the room.

Finally, forty minutes went by and she still hadn't come back. I looked at Matt and motioned to the stairs. When we got to the top of the stairs, the attic seemed a bit darker than it was previously. We walked through the first room and made our way to the bedroom. I slowly opened the door and peeked inside. There was Laura lying in bed. I said, "Hey Laura, it's just us." There was no response. I said it again. Still no response. As I looked a little closer, I realized she was fast asleep. I looked at Matt and started to laugh. That was a new one on me. I've had people fall asleep when I do my presentations, but never when they were bait on an investigation.

When we entered the room, I caught a brief glimpse of something moving. It looked like a shadow. There were no lights on in the room, so this threw me for a loop. There was a light source behind me coming from the stairway. Initially, I thought the shadow belonged to me, and that it was most likely caused by the light coming from behind me. What makes me think that it was not my shadow was the fact that I was standing still and the shadow was moving from left to right at the foot of the bed.

I wasn't sure if we should wake Laura or not. I didn't want to just grab my stuff and leave without her knowing. After pondering what to do, I decided that we should probably go ahead and wake her up. I purposely made a noise and she jumped up and started rubbing the sleep from her eyes. I asked if George had been around and she said she felt his presence earlier, but it felt like he was gone now. At this point I couldn't wait to watch the video footage to see if it had captured anything unusual.

We went back downstairs and talked some more. I asked Laura if she felt tired prior to going up to the bedroom. She said she wasn't at all that tired; there was just something about that room that made her doze off. I've encountered something similar at the First Unitarian Church in Alton. What if whatever is in certain rooms drains you of energy? Almost like what happens on Thanksgiving when you eat turkey and feel sleepy afterwards. One second you're fine, and the next you're exhausted and drooling in front of the television. Perhaps George, in an effort to manifest, is pulling energy from whoever is in the room. It's hard to say for sure; I'm just tossing around some ideas.

When I got the opportunity to review the video footage, it was very tedious. I usually have to set aside blocks of time over several days to effectively review all the evidence from an investigation. I don't have the patience to do it all in one sitting because I start losing focus very quickly. I would hate to miss something important because I started thinking about other things, like the meaning of life or how tired I am. Not much happened throughout the hour and a half of tape. However, there were a few things worth mentioning.

First, there were knocking noises captured several times on the tape. It could just be the house settling. The sounds were similar to someone knocking on a door or a wall. When I think of house-settling noises, they're more like creaks, and maybe one knocking sound. They usually don't sound live four or five knocks in a row.

Secondly, there was one instance where it appears the blanket on the bed moved just a little bit. It can't decide whether it moved because Laura was under it, or because something was lying down on top of it. It was dark, and infrared light doesn't show everything like you wish it would. Lastly, Laura fell asleep extraordinarily quickly. She entered the room, sat down on the bed for a minute, then lay down and covered up. Three minutes after that, she was out.

There were a few other instances of some strange sounds captured on the video halfway through. Lasting only a few seconds, you can hear what sounds like someone walking on a wood floor. You can hear creaks, and the sounds of shoes hitting the floor as they take five or six steps. Unfortunately, it only lasts a few seconds, and since there were multiple people in the house, it could have been one of them moving about. However, I know for certain that Matt and I didn't move from the dining room table, and Laura's mom was sitting on the couch watching television the whole time we were waiting for Laura to come back downstairs.

One other thing that was captured on the videotape was the sound of a moan. A lot of times, when you capture audio that may have a ghostly origin, it is not very clear. This moan was clear and lasted a couple of seconds. It may have just been Laura snoring or making some other kind of sleep noise. She did move a bit when it happened, so that's a sign to me that she may have been the cause.

Other than these few things, the video was not very exciting. That's a price we have to pay with real-life paranormal investigating. It's not at all like it is on TV. Exciting things seem to happen a lot more often on paranormal television shows than they do in real life. Maybe it's because ghosts like to perform when they know it will boost ratings. Who am I to judge?

I can't say for sure that the house is haunted. I can't say that it's not haunted, either. Multiple people have experienced what they feel to be ghostly activity there. Just because the spirits didn't make themselves known to us when we were there, doesn't mean they aren't there. They just didn't come out to play when we were there. I would like to go back again sometime, but I was informed weeks before writing this that the house is going to be up for sale soon. If that's the case, I would be curious to know if the new owners will have any experiences up in the time-portal bedroom with old George. Only time will tell.

Update:

Sadly, Laura passed away in 2013 before this book was published. Rest in Peace, Laura.

6. The Tag-Along Ghost

The father of a friend of my family's contacted me because he had some paranormal activity occur at a couple of different residences in the Mascoutah area. To protect his anonymity, I'll call him Ron. He told me he doesn't mind my using his real name but I prefer not to.

Ron and his wife moved into a house on the south end of Mascoutah in 1975. The house was built in the 1930s. It was a small two-bedroom home, just the right size for a young couple. Later in 1975, the family began to grow. Their first child was born in December and a second one came along in 1977. The bedroom that Ron and his wife shared was towards the front of the house while the kids' bedroom was in the back, off the kitchen.

The home had experienced a tragedy prior to Ron's arrival. Neighbors told him about a married couple that lived there previously who were going through some tough times. The husband had a bad drinking problem and the wife began having an affair. One night, the husband left the house and never came back. His body was found later that night, and although his death was ruled an accident, some thought it was suicide. Perhaps this man's spirit is what caused the paranormal experiences Ron had inside the home.

The first story Ron related to me occurred prior to their first child being born. He and his wife were lying in bed, ready for a nice rest after a long, hard day. Ron's wife was asleep and Ron was lying on his back with his arms crossed over his stomach. As he lay there, he looked towards the foot of the bed and saw a shape. It was humanlike, although all he could make out was a head and broad shoulders. The rest of the figure was hazy and faded away the farther down it went. As far as the face goes, he could only see the eyes, which looked black and empty. Ron was terrified. He tried to move but couldn't. Eventually, he was able to scream. As he did, the figure disappeared. His wife woke up immediately, but she saw nothing.

Definitely not the Gingerbread Man

The above photo is a sketch of what Ron saw that night. If you see it, do not try to apprehend it. This spirit may be armed (although it doesn't appear to have any arms) and could quite possibly be dangerous. If you see it, just scream and run around in circles with your arms raised above your head.

Ron swears he wasn't dreaming. He wasn't even asleep at that point. Whatever it was, it was standing at the foot of the bed, staring at him and his wife. To me, this is one of the scariest things I can imagine. Think of all the spooky things that could be watching you in your home without you even being aware they are there! Think about the times you heard people talk about seeing a ghost. When they saw the ghost, they were awake. Now consider the fact that about one-third of your life is spent asleep. Just because you are sleeping, it doesn't mean the ghosts are on break. That's a prime time for them to materialize and just *watch*. Watch you as you lay asleep, blissfully unaware that there is a ghost in the room with you. That's a terrifying thought.

After you finish this chapter, go ahead and put the book down. Try going to sleep. Don't forget to turn off the lights so it's completely dark. That way, if anything materializes at the foot of your bed, you'll be less likely to know it's standing there with its dark, empty eyes, sharp, pointy teeth, long, blood-encrusted fingernails, and its terribly hungry stomach.

For those who can't go to sleep now, I'll continue the story.

A second incident in the house happened in November of 1977. Ron had some medical issues at the time and was on leave from work.

One cold evening, Ron grabbed two notes from his doctor off the kitchen table. The notes were to present to his boss to show that he was, indeed, ill. He wanted to read up on his condition, so he went to the bookshelf and took out a medical encyclopedia. He then took the notes and the book into the bedroom, where he sat on the bed reading about his illness. As he read, he got an uneasy feeling that he needed to leave the room. He put the notes in the book to mark the place he left off reading and left the room. When he came back for the book, the notes were gone.

Ron, his wife, and the two children were the only ones in the house. The children were with the wife when this happened. The youngest was only seven months old, and the oldest was not yet two. Ron went through the book twice, page by page, but was unable to locate the missing notes. He looked on the bed, under the bed, in the trash, in his pockets and still couldn't find them. He never did find them.

Ron and his family moved out of that house before the end of 1977. They bought an old farmhouse, also located in Mascoutah. This home was on the outskirts south of town. Ron's brother-in-law moved in with them and paid rent to help out.

After some of the things that had happened to him at his previous home, Ron was starting to pay attention when things just didn't seem right. He noticed that the last family to rent the farmhouse only stayed six months. Digging a little deeper, he found that most of the previous occupants hadn't stayed very long. This put up a red flag in his mind. He had a feeling that something was wrong with the home. He knew in the back of his mind that he was probably going to find out what it was before too long.

The house was old and drafty. It was small and didn't have very good ventilation. The well water tasted horrible and the house just didn't have much appeal. Women didn't like to be there by themselves, for some reason. Times were tough though, so they needed to make the best of it. The plus side was that the property had a lot of acreage where Ron could hunt. The yard was big enough to allow the family's dogs to run freely, as well.

The house had one bedroom and it was upstairs. In fact, the entire upstairs was one large bedroom with a couple of closets and a few windows. The room held the bed that Ron and his wife shared, their daughter's bed and their son's crib. To get there, you would go through the kitchen, open a door, go up a creepy stairway and come up through the floor of the bedroom. The stairway had a three-foot wall along it to prevent anyone from falling.

Shortly after moving into the farmhouse, the family was playing a board game in the living room. The youngest child was upstairs taking a nap in his crib. Ron heard a banging noise come from the bedroom and assumed that his son was awake. He went upstairs to retrieve the boy, but he was still sound asleep when Ron approached the crib. Ron went back downstairs to continue the game when the banging started again. Ron went upstairs a second time and found his son was still asleep. From the way he was lying in the crib, the baby wouldn't have been able to kick the sides to make the banging noise.

Ron went back downstairs, and sure enough, the banging started again. This time Ron went into ninja mode and crept quietly up the stairs. All the while, the banging noise was still coming from the bedroom. When he reached the top of the stairs, he hid behind the three-foot wall and listened. The banging was still going on. As soon as Ron moved to peek over the wall, the noise stopped. The baby was still lying in the center of the crib, fast asleep. Puzzled, but not particularly alarmed, Ron went back downstairs.

Once downstairs, the banging started for the fourth time. This time, Ron took his brother-in-law up to the bedroom with him. They sneaked up the stairs as the sounds were still emanating from the bedroom. Again, as soon as they peered past the wall at the top of the stairs, the noises stopped. This time, Ron had enough. He grabbed his son and took him downstairs, where he finished his nap on the couch.

They never heard the noises again after that night. To this day, Ron can't explain what was causing them.

On another occasion, Ron was in the basement doing some work. He heard the door to the basement open, and his son suddenly came tumbling down the stairs. Once at the bottom, the boy hit an ironing board that was leaning up against the wall. Had the ironing board not been there, he would have smashed into a brick wall. The child wasn't even two years old when this happened. He was too small to reach the handle of the basement door, and yet the door somehow opened.

The family experienced a lot of setbacks while living in the farmhouse. Some things were explainable and some weren't. Ron feels that the house had no soul and was the cause of a lot of their pain and struggles. He also feels that the house didn't want his family living there.

Over the course of their time in the home, they lost three dogs. One was run over by a tractor. They had a Doberman pinscher that just disappeared, as did a third dog, a beagle. Perhaps they ran away, or were stolen. Maybe coyotes got them. Either way, the family's pets were gone and the house was deemed responsible.

The family found themselves getting sick quite often. The house was cold and damp, which may have caused some of the sickness. The bad-tasting well water may have been the culprit for the violent bouts with diarrhea and vomiting that they experienced during their time in the house.

The property around the house had a bad vibe to it. The woods where Ron hunted were spooky, and Ron would often feel as if he wasn't alone when he walked through them. Ron recalled hunting squirrels one day when he got a very uneasy feeling. It ran chills up his spine and he decided to call the hunt off.

The family didn't stay outside very long during evenings. They made it a habit to be inside well before dark because of the strange ambience the yard held.

They finally moved out after living there for about fourteen months. At their new home, things were peaceful. There wasn't a dark, brooding feeling hovering over the family anymore. Although, at one point, Ron though he heard his name called when he was home alone, so perhaps the haunting wasn't over quite yet. I wonder if the spirit had been following them around from house to house. Perhaps, since they moved three times in about four years, the ghost couldn't keep up any longer and decided to go bother someone else. Or maybe it liked the farmhouse and stayed there to wait for a new family to move in.

7. Alton Hauntings Tour - Revisited

The Alton Hauntings tours have been incredible since my last book, *The Lighter Side of Darkness.* As I began laying out the stories for this book, I really wanted to update the tour stories. I didn't want to repeat everything, either. There have been so many amazing things that have happened on the tour that it's hard not to include them all, but that would be impossible. So, without further ado, here's a very, very, *very* updated version of the tour stories from *The Lighter Side of Darkness."*

Enos Sanitorium

This massive building was built as a home for wealthy farm implement manufacturer Nathaniel Hanson in 1857. It stands high on a bluff overlooking the Mississippi River. At first glance, the mansion was Hanson's way of showing off his wealth by providing an impressive home for his family, but the house had another, hidden purpose: It was designed to help runaway slaves escape to freedom on the Underground Railroad.

Although the upper part of the building is beautiful, it was the basement that truly made this place special. Under the front yard was a specially designed tunnel that ran fifteen feet below the street. I use the term tunnel loosely, as it was more of a long, narrow room with an arched ceiling. I am not sure how many slaves would have been kept hidden in this room, nor am I sure how long they would have been there. I'd have to assume the answers would be as many as could fit and however long it took.

The former Enos Sanatorium

During this time, people who were caught helping escaped slaves would often be lynched in their own front yards as a warning to other abolitionists who might feel tempted to do the same. They'd be beaten, hanged, whatever it took to get the message across. Slaves were considered nothing more than expensive farm machinery. They weren't human; they were property. If you were caught with another man's property, you were stealing. This was considered the law back then, and many people were abused and murdered for aiding escaped slaves.

In order to avoid being caught, the Hanson family came up with a system to let the slaves know when it was safe to come to the house. On top of the building was a large cupola. If it was safe, the Hansons would place a single lantern in one of the cupola windows. If there was danger, two lanterns would be placed in the window. As the slaves would approach the river, they'd look up at the building on top of the bluff and know instantly if they should advance or stay put. If there was a single light in the window, they'd make their way across the river and into the Hansons' carriage house. From there, they would be escorted into a tunnel that led to the sub-basement holding area. There they would stay until it was safe to move on to the next stop on the road to freedom.

The Hanson family made it through the slavery years without ever being caught. The house stayed in the family's possession until around 1911, when it was purchased by Dr. W.H. Enos.

Dr. Enos used the building as a tuberculosis sanatorium during his tenure in Alton. It seemed to be more of a rest home, as there was no cure for TB at that time. Patients would spend most of their days next to the open windows. They would also spend a lot of time eating good, rich, wholesome food. Fresh air and good nutrition were the only things that could be done at the time to fight the disease. Dr. Enos ended up losing around a hundred patients during each of his first three years running the sanatorium. He decided to try and remedy the situation by literally "raising the roof" on the old building.

In 1914, Dr. Enos had the roof lifted up off the building and added a third story. By doing this, he would be able to care for more patients. He also added a wing to the side of the sanatorium to house his staff of doctors and nurses so they would be available at all hours. Dr. Enos was well-intentioned, but by adding on the extra floor, it only increased the amount of patients who died in the building. He held onto the sanatorium for about ten years until it was sold and converted into apartments. It has been a series of apartment buildings ever since.

This is the point where the ghost stories began to develop. Tenants in the building have experienced a steady flow of strange occurrences, including having doors open and close, lights turn on and off, and the sound of disembodied voices. It seemed that most often, these things would happen when the building was being renovated. Perhaps the spirits don't want their home to change. It could be that renovating old buildings releases spirits into our realm. We may never know, but there have been reports from many different places of renovations triggering paranormal activity.

We are not sure who is haunting this place. Could it be the slaves that traveled through here on their way to safety? We are very fortunate to know from local history that this building was part of the Underground Railroad, since it was generally too dangerous for the people who helped escaped slaves to keep written records. Due to the lack of details about the Hanson family's participation in the Underground Railroad, we don't know if any slaves died in the basement room or elsewhere on the property. I'm not saying that you need a death for a place to be haunted, but that is usually the case. I am sure that regardless of whether any slaves died there, this building still houses a lot of their emotions. Whether it's hunger, fear, sickness, sadness or pain, these feelings got soaked up into the stone that lines the tunnel walls. The walls will speak, if only we would take the time to listen.

I think a bigger cause of this building being haunted is due to the high number of patients who died here during its tenure as a TB sanatorium. These people also suffered, and I am sure they left their emotional energy in the building, as well. Since the patient rooms are now apartments, it seems to be logical that the patients are the ones causing the upstairs activity.

The Enos doesn't seem to be generating as much paranormal activity as it did in the past, but we occasionally get tenants who come out and relay their stories to us about something unexplained that happened in their part of the building the week before. Since we only go into the basement area, we are a bit limited with what experiences we can have. Here are some of those experiences:

Shadowy figures have been the most common thing I've come across. They aren't as frequent as what I'd like. Maybe on one in every three tours someone will spot a shadowy figure. I've seen them at times, and sometimes those around me get the opportunity. We had one of those instances just this past year where a girl standing off to the right of me started freaking out because she saw a shadow walk right in front of her. When I tell the basement story, I turn out all the lights, so it gets very dark down there. To see a shadow move in a room that's already dark seems very odd. Once you witness it, it's hard not to get a bit creeped out by it. I've had people scream, jump, and grab my arm as hard as they could in response to seeing these shadows.

Every once in a while, the Enos shadows will make contact through some form of touch. We had people see a shadow and then feel a cold breeze. Sometimes, they've had their hair played with, or their shoulder touched. On one tour, we had a girl who saw a shadow, and then it went away. Seconds later, she felt something smack her on the backside. With it being dark in the basement, you have to wonder if it was a ghost or just some frisky person on the tour.

During the 2012 tours, several people had experiences in the tunnel. I noticed one girl was starting to get a bit antsy in the back of the room. At one point during the story, she let out a scream, and then a girl next to her started yelling at me to turn a light on. Everyone's eyes were wide when the light came on. Once I got everyone calmed down, the girl who screamed said she felt someone touch her face. She screamed because she knew there was nobody in front of her at the time who could have done it. The person standing next to her said that when the girl screamed, she saw something move past her. She said it was a dark shape, but she couldn't see any details due to the room being in darkness.

Also in 2012, after finishing my stories, I made my way out of the tunnel and towards the stairway door so I could point people in the right direction for leaving the building. While standing there, I noticed a mother and daughter hurrying past me. The daughter was in tears and looked very upset. I asked the mom if the girl was okay, and she smiled and nodded as she made her way past me. Once outside, the mother and daughter came up to me. The daughter asked if I had bumped into her while I was telling the stories. She was standing next to me and felt something bump into her. It wasn't me; I was about five feet from her. Generally, when I accidentally bump into someone during a tour, I speak up and tell them I did it. That way, nobody thinks it was something paranormal. In this case, it probably *was* paranormal.

In 2010, my "caboose" Chasidy had a frightening experience. A caboose's job is to stay at the back of the tour group to round up stragglers. She told me her story several times, but to truly get it right, I had her write it out for me. Here's the story straight from Chasidy:

I have had the opportunity to be the caboose on the Alton Hauntings Tour with Luke many times in the past. It is always a great time, and I never get tired of hearing the stories of the rich history this town offers. I have had my fair share of experiences on these tours, but I am reluctant to share with the group. I never want people to think that Luke and I are creating stories or experiences just so that people feel this is the "real deal." However, what happened to me in the fall of 2010 on this tour deserves to be shared.

We were at one of my favorite stops on the tour -- the Enos. Not only is this place associated with the Underground Railroad, which makes it amazing in itself, but it is also a stop where we get to go inside. Luke will lead the group down to the basement, which contains a tunnel believed to have been a place where slaves would hide until it was safe to move farther along. To set the mood of the story and the history, Luke will turn off his lantern and begin speaking. This is where my personal story begins.

71

When we go into the room, I always bring up the rear. Luke will have everyone go as far as he can into the tunnel and once everyone is settled he'll turn off the tunnel light and come in with his lit lantern. Luke will then stand along one of the walls in the center of the room. I'll enter the room at this time and stand with my back in front of the doorway.

As a person who has been on this tour many, many times, I have heard these stories many, many times. It has become kind of my own game to see if I can mouth the words to the story. However, there was a new addition to the story that night. Had it not been for this, my story might never have happened. Luke started off by saying, "I am going to turn off the lights and there will be a glow floating below the tunnel ceiling. It is not an orb, it was just an energy efficient bulb and they do that for a bit when you turn them off." So I focused on the soft glow of the light as he began to speak, waiting to play my game. What I saw next was something I will never forget.

I saw what appeared to be a large shadow engulf the soft glow. I was panicking a bit, but did not want to interrupt him or cause a riot when 25-30 people started running for an exit. I just kept an eye on it and kept thinking, "I'm okay. Luke sees stuff like this and doesn't freak out. It's not going to hurt me. This will make a good story to share on the way back home." Unfortunately, my bravery soon disappeared as the shadowy cloud moved and was now behind me by my left shoulder. It was at this point that I began to just cry and cry and beg Luke to turn on the lights. He had to escort me out of the basement. I went outside, sat on the steps, tears streaming down, and just overwhelmed at what I had personally experienced.

There is really no way to describe the feeling I had when that figure was behind me. It was a mixture of fear and overwhelming sadness, definitely not something I had ever experienced before. I know that there are lots of people who are skeptics, but there is no one who can convince me that this experience was anything less than paranormal.

Now is a good time to tell my version because there is more to the story. First off, I was looking great that night and was on my game. Chasidy failed to mention that in her story. I just want to make sure I am painting this picture fairly. I was telling the story, not even realizing that Chasidy was having an experience. Suddenly, mid-story, I hear someone crying and pleading for me to turn the light on. When I turned the lantern on and looked towards the sound of crying, I realized it was Chasidy. I asked if she was okay and she couldn't even answer. I asked if she needed to go outside and she shook her head yes. I set my lantern down and rushed to take her out. At this point, Chasidy had her head down, and I was dragging her out of the room. I thought I was leading us out, but there was something in front of us.

Whatever was behind Chasidy would have been in the doorway. When I started to walk her out, we had to leave the room, walk through a couple of other rooms, make a right, make another right, make a left and then we would be at the stairs leading to the outside door. As we made our way through the first two rooms, there was a shelving unit with some outdoor supplies on it. There were two decorative flags draped over the unit. As we approached the second room, those flags started moving back and forth, as if a breeze were causing them to move. It happened right in front of us. Chasidy didn't see it since she was still looking down. I wanted to bring it to her attention, but Chasidy was so freaked out that I didn't dare mention that there was more happening. I didn't feel any kind of breeze or anything that would have caused the flags to move. It's my opinion that whatever was showing Chasidy attention that night decided to leave the room ahead of us.

One of my favorite things that happened in the Enos occurred a few years back. When I get to the point in my story-telling when I mention that sometimes people feel the sensation of being touched, I generally pause. It's during this time that one can sometimes hear the swift smack of a male tour guest getting punched by the female he attempted to scare.

The Enos tunnel. There appears to be a misty, bluish figure at the back of the tunnel with what appear to be a pair of dark boots at the bottom. (photo by Ben Deshon)

On one occasion I left the pause a drag out bit too long. Unfortunately, we had a gentleman who was having a bout with gas, and he was unable to hold it any longer. Rather than wait until I began speaking again to at least give him some sound cover, he let it rip at a moment when it was absolutely quit, making the entire group erupt in laughter.

One other incident that happened during a tour at the Enos wasn't paranormal but it was definitely odd. A couple of years ago, I was waiting for everyone to finish taking pictures in the tunnel. I was standing in one of the other basement rooms when something made me look down. I noticed something silver colored buried in a dusty crack where the wall and floor met. When I bent down and wiped the debris away, I saw it was a silver charm bracelet. Looking closer, I found that the charms were all in the shapes of boys' and girl's heads. Each one had a name engraved on it. I don't know if it was old, but judging by the names, they weren't typical of the 1800s, so I think the bracelet was more recent. I didn't keep it; I hid it in the Enos. Every time I did a tour, I would check the hiding spot. The last time I checked, the bracelet was gone. Maybe its owner claimed it, or maybe it was some sticky-fingered person on the tour. Then again, perhaps a ghost took it. I guess I'll never know.

Other Random Locations

Another puzzling thing that happened on one of my tours occurred in a little corner garden. The location where we stop isn't haunted, as far as I know, which makes what happened there a few years back difficult to explain.

I stopped the tour so everyone could sit down while I told a couple of stories. One of the locations I talk about at this point is the former Mansion House, which unfortunately burned down in January 2010. I also talk about the Franklin House. We don't stand in front because it's surrounded by bars. The tours tend to attract patrons from the bars and it causes a disturbance.

During this fall tour, we stopped at the garden and everyone was surrounding me in a large circle. About five minutes into my talk, I heard a commotion coming up the sidewalk towards us. The garden is on a corner of a popular intersection, and even though I couldn't see who was making the commotion, I knew they were heading our way. Seconds later, two couples approached us. One of them was arguing loudly. This caused a disruption with the tour, making it hard to keep everyone focused on what I was saying.

Once the unhappy couple got past us, they crossed the street and turned right. From where I was standing, I was looking right at them. Anybody standing behind me could also see them. Once across the street, the couple stopped and began to really have it out. At one point, the guy actually hit the girl. When I saw that, I stopped talking for a second, not only because I couldn't believe it, but also because I had to try to keep the guys on the tour from getting involved.

The squabbling couple moved a few feet down the sidewalk and stopped again. I had turned towards my group to try to keep going on with the story. When I looked back at the couple, I noticed an older gentleman was staring at them. He wore what looked like an old brown suit and was standing not six feet from where they had first stopped. When I noticed him, I immediately started thinking, *please, don't get involved.* I turned towards the tour to continue the story, and then looked back at the old guy to make sure he hadn't stepped in to defend the girl. The couple was still standing there arguing, but there was no sign of the old man. Eventually, the couple moved on.

As we walked to the next stop, a group of four people caught up to me and asked if I saw the old guy standing across the street. They said they saw him and then all of sudden he was gone. At this point, I started thinking that he had moved very swiftly for a person his age. When we got to the next location, I asked if anyone else had seen him. Nobody else had. The strange thing about this is that of the forty people on the tour, at least one-third to one-half of them would have been looking directly across the street at the fighting couple. So why did only five of us see this older gentleman? Furthermore, how did he disappear so quickly? I think this falls into the category of, "How do you know you haven't ever seen a ghost?"

There are so many haunted locations in Alton that we can't cover all of them in one night. I try and get a feel for the crowd and tailor the stories according to what they are into. However, I noticed this past year that sometimes stories present themselves. For example, I don't always talk about the Cracker Factory, but I did during one October tour in 2012. While I was telling the story, some patrons were looking at the building. Several of them started pointing, and sure enough, you could see someone standing in one of the windows. Several people, including myself, saw someone standing there. No sooner did we see him than he vanished in front of us. The neat thing about this is that the building had been empty for a couple of years. There should not have been anyone inside.

One evening while walking past the old Sparks Milling Company office building, heading towards the Illinois State Penitentiary site, we had something happen to a handful of us walking in the lead of the tour group. As we were walking, I mentioned to the people around me that the Sparks building was haunted. I said it's not part of the tour, but if anyone wanted to hear the story, I'd be happy to tell it. As we looked at the building, it sounded like the front door opened and slammed shut. We knew full well the door didn't move, but the sound was very loud. All I could say was, "See, told you it was haunted!"

One would think that the people of Alton would be used to our tour groups walking through town, but it never ceases to amaze me to see the reactions we get from people driving by. Some of them don't pay attention to what they're doing because they're so busy gawking at us. We've seen cars go off the road and in one case, rear-end another car. This past year, I was walking a group of fifty people up the street towards one of our stops. Some people who weren't on the tour got to the corner at the same time my group did. They stopped and asked if we were a history tour. I said no, we were actually on our way to a lynching. They were welcome to join us if they brought their own pitchforks and torches!

All in all, the tours have been a blast. Someone reports experiencing something unusual at some point during almost every tour. In some cases, it may just be nerves. However, there's always a chance that we may be joined by one of the departed inhabitants of one of the most haunted small towns in America: Alton, Illinois.

8. Heads-Up Cemetery

I am usually not big on romping around a cemetery in the middle of the night. Although cemeteries are peaceful and serene, I think it's a bit disrespectful to intrude on those who lay at rest below your feet. That's not to say that I have not done it. I've actually had some wonderful experiences investigating cemeteries, but I always show the upmost respect to those whose places of rest I am intruding upon. One must also remember that even though the dead are said to be buried six feet under, that wasn't always a hard-and-fast rule. Remember that the next time you go off the beaten path and venture close to grave markers. I am six feet tall and my arms are about thirty-two inches long. If someone my size were buried about two feet underground, that would leave about eight inches of arm length to reach above the ground. That's more than enough to grab at the feet of unsuspecting cemetery visitors.

Years ago, I had the opportunity to investigate a cemetery in the St. Louis area. I don't want to go into specifics as far as its name or location because I do not want to inspire people to go out there in droves and cause damage to the property. Not that my fellow ghost hunters would do something like that, but there are others who would. So for the purpose of anonymity, and since Troy Taylor already uses "Graveyard X" for one of his locations, we are going to call this location "Cemetery E" That's mainly because when I was in grade school and we learned how to spell cemetery, my teacher said, "How do you leave a cemetery? With Eeeeeee's." (With ease.) Thus, we learned that the word cemetery has all e's for the vowels. I still remember that little trick.

When the paranormal team and I went out to investigate the cemetery, it was in the fall and very chilly outside. It was late at night, and we intended on only staying for only a couple of hours. There was a new person with us who claimed to have psychic abilities. This was to be her first investigation with us.

For those who know me, I am very skeptical of certain things. Psychic abilities are one of them. That's not to say they don't exist. I do believe that it's possible someone can have those kinds of abilities. In my years of being in this field, I have met a ton of individuals who claimed to be psychic, and only a few have amazed me. I was going to keep an open mind, though, and try my best to not judge her without giving her a fair chance to dazzle me with her powers.

She met up with a couple of our members, and they rode together to Cemetery E. She wasn't told anything about where we were going or what we knew about the location. She was coming into to this investigation completely blind. We figured this would be a great way to test her abilities. If she could pinpoint certain areas that we knew were hotspots, then perhaps she was legit.

Cemetery E was built in the mid-1860s. It covers almost 100 acres, and has several mausoleums and crypts. The terrain is hilly and is covered with beautiful old trees. The surrounding homes are large and are getting a bit rundown. It was definitely a place I could enjoy visiting during the daytime. A year later, I did just that. I wouldn't recommend going there at night because the area is somewhat dangerous.

We knew of several stories of hauntings at Cemetery E. We had experienced several unusual occurrences ourselves on previous visits. There were many others that we heard about from people who were at the cemetery visiting the graves of loved ones.

One of the tales takes place around a hillside. There had been multiple reports of the spirit of a young boy who looks very much alive and who appears to be having a lot of fun as he weaves in and out of the trees and tombstones. His trusty sidekick, a dog, follows him wherever he goes. They are playing together and appear to be having a great time being young and full of energy.

This boy and dog have been seen by multiple people. One person I talked to mentioned that she and her sister were in the cemetery early one morning visiting the burial site of some of their family members. While they were kneeling in front of the grave, they started hearing a child laughing and a dog barking. They were in the middle of praying and found it rude that a child would be playing in the cemetery. They finished their prayers with the sound of laughter filling the background. They stood up and tried to find out where the child was, but they could see no one. They looked all over, but to no avail.

They thought maybe it was a kid from one of the houses around the cemetery, but the more they thought about it, the less likely it seemed. They were a distance from the nearest house and the laughing child and barking dog sounded as if they were right next to them. They said this was the only time they ever experienced anything like that in the cemetery.

Hill where the boy and dog have been seen
(Photo by Zach A.)

A second witness I spoke with mentioned that they saw a dog walking among some tombstones. It looked healthy but was whimpering as if it were sad. The boy wasn't around this time, only the dog. The cemetery visitors felt bad for the dog, and they tried to go to it and show it some attention. Every time they got near, it would run off. They assumed it was shy or afraid. At one point, they saw it run behind a tree. They thought it must have stopped and sat down because they didn't see it come out. They quietly crept over to the tree so they could approach the dog gently. To their surprise, it was nowhere to be found. There was nowhere for it to go, but it had disappeared. The visitors even looked up in the tree just in case the dog had somehow managed to scale it.

They had never heard any stories about ghosts haunting the cemetery, so they didn't think much of it at the time. Later, they heard about some of the unusual experiences other people had at the cemetery. It was then they realized they had seen a ghost dog.

We knew about the sightings of this boy and dog. Some of our team members had experienced the phenomenon on earlier visits. That evening I definitely heard what I thought was a dog whimpering, but I didn't know if it was coming from inside the cemetery or from one of the neighboring houses. I thought that perhaps my mind was playing tricks on me, since I knew the story of the boy and his dog. I think in times of anticipation or fear, we can make ourselves see and hear things that aren't really there.

When our new psychic member started walking around the cemetery, we deliberately stayed behind her. We didn't want to lead her to any of the known hotspots. At one point, she started laughing and said, "Well, that's not something you see every day!" She said she saw a boy and a dog running along one of the hills. We immediately looked at each other and thought this was a good sign. No one else in our group saw them. Hearing what she was describing took the investigation to a whole different level than what we were accustomed to. But our experience on that chilly, fall evening was about to get even better for everyone involved.

She started to walk over to where she saw the spirits of the boy and the dog. I noticed that she was still smiling.

She insisted that she could still see them playing. Once we got up on the hillside, she began to walk at a slower pace. We asked if she still saw them. She said she didn't. She continued walking slowly past the row of tombstones. She stopped in front of one of the markers and pointed at it. We discovered that a boy was buried in that spot along with his dog. The inscription didn't say how he died. If I remember correctly, the boy was less than ten years old. We now had a grave marker that tied in perfectly with the ghostly encounters.

On one of my return visits, I spent some time in the area of the boy's grave. I walked around for a while but didn't hear, see or feel anything I could deem as being paranormal. I knew the area where they were buried from the last time we were there, but I was having difficulty locating the exact spot. It's funny how different things look during the day than they do at night. It's kind of like when I go hunting. When I am trying to locate my deer stand, I can do it very easily in the daylight, but at night, I get turned around a lot and lose my bearings.

Since I couldn't find the exact location of the marker, I decided to just sit and take a rest in the general vicinity of where I recalled them being buried. I picked a large tombstone and sat with my back against it. I am sure it would have really freaked someone out if they had walked up on me sitting there by myself, especially if they approached from behind the tombstone and I suddenly rose into view. I probably sat there for fifteen minutes before I closed my eyes and really began to relax. I may have dozed off at one point, because what happened next still seems very surreal.

I don't remember exactly how the events transpired because I was in a state of complete relaxation where I was half asleep. All I remember is sitting there and feeling something on my leg. For a moment I though I was at home, and reached out to pet my dog. The dog's head was resting gently on my thigh and I could even feel it breathing as I petted it. My eyes were closed but at one point, it felt like the dog lifted its head to look at me and then laid its head back down. When I opened my eyes, I looked down and nothing was there. My hand was still making a petting motion inches above my leg, but I no longer felt anything resting there.

I was confused at first because I was still in a bit of a sleepy daze. It took me a few minutes to put everything together. Whether or not it was the ghost dog or just a dream remains to be determined. However, given where I was sitting and the feeling I had of actually petting a dog, it's hard for me to deny the fact that I may have been visited by someone's pet from beyond the grave. The boy didn't make an appearance, at least not that I know of. Maybe he was sitting on one of the nearby grave markers, keeping a watchful eye on his dog and the stranger who was petting it.

When I was at the cemetery for the investigation, I wondered off on my own for awhile. I came across a tombstone that contained a photo of the person who was buried in that spot. The photo was oval in shape and was enclosed in glass. Unfortunately, it had been badly damaged. At first, I thought maybe it was done by accident. Perhaps a lawnmower shot a rock at it or something. The damage was to the person's face, so I felt that it may have been done intentionally. I don't like to speculate, but it almost seemed as if whoever did it hated the person in the photo.

I sat down by the grave and began to talk to the person buried there. Normally, I don't do that, but I did feel bad about the damage and was curious if I could use that topic as a way to open communication with a spirit. I had my digital recorder running to try and capture any voices that I was unable to hear while I was asking the questions. When I listened to the recording later, there was a spot where it gets completely overrun by static. It was the first time my recorder ever did that. I tried to clean it up, but was unable to. I was hoping that maybe there would be a voice embedded behind the static, but there was just too much static to identify anything that might be underneath it. The static happened after I asked if the man who was buried there was upset that his photo had been damaged. Perhaps the static was his way of saying that he was very unhappy with the situation.

When I returned to the cemetery, I was unable to relocate the tombstone with the defaced photograph. I was hoping to talk to the man whose grave it was again, and ask him to speak more clearly this time.

Another location in the cemetery that deserves mentioning is a little more frightening. Our new psychic member picked up on it very quickly. We were walking towards some trees, and as we approached, she mentioned that we might want to keep our heads up. When we asked why, she began to tell us about an angry spirit who tries to hit people with rocks. What she didn't know what that we had already heard about that ghost and she absolutely nailed his location!

Several of our team members had experienced this in different ways. Sometimes, as you are walking through that part of the cemetery, you could hear things crashing around you, but you would never see what it was that was making the sound. Other times, you may actually see rocks falling from the sky. The third, and most painful way to experience the spirits, is when you begin to actually be pelted by rocks that seem to come from nowhere. The spirit can be eerily accurate with his aim.

Aside from the members of our team, I was only able to find one other witness who had a similar story. They were visiting the cemetery with a couple of other people on a summer day. They were in the middle of the cemetery and were walking along a row of tombstones when one of the guys in their group grabbed his leg. When the others asked if he was okay, he said that something had hit him. A rock lay on the ground near where he was standing. The area on his leg where he was struck was very red, and eventually it became badly bruised. They looked all around to find out who the culprit was, but they didn't see anyone. They assumed the rock was thrown by someone from one of the houses around the cemetery. Perhaps that person used a slingshot. If so, their aim was uncanny.

Tree where rocks are thrown at unsuspecting cemetery visitors (Photo by Zach A.)

I haven't been back to the cemetery in quite some time. Maybe someday I will return. Now that I am more into doing research, I can try and trace the boy's name on the tombstone to see whether he and his dog lost their lives together, or if the dog was buried there later. Understanding what happened to them might help their spirits find peace.

Although I purposely didn't disclose the real name of Cemetery E, if you ever go wandering around an old cemetery and find yourself struck by a flying rock, congratulations! You may have found the secret location. Your prize? A nice lump on the old noggin.

On a side note from the cemetery investigation, but one related to our psychic recruit, I'll mention another incident. For many years, I was having difficulty sleeping at night. I would lie in bed, looking up at the ceiling and waiting for sleep to overtake me. Sometimes it would take hours for unconsciousness to finally grab hold. My sleeplessness was definitely caused by stress from work and life in general.

On one occasion, as I was lying in bed next to the sleeping wife, I was really having trouble falling asleep. I was very stressed out from work, and it was taking a toll on me. I remember looking at the clock and seeing that it was 2:08 a.m. I looked back at the ceiling and tiredly closed my eyes. All of a sudden, I got a weird feeling that something was hovering above me. It felt like I was being watched. I opened my eyes and found that I was indeed being watched. Floating above me was a woman. She wore a white gown and looked very real. She had long, brown hair and had a beautiful, peaceful expression on her lovely face. I'd be lying if I didn't say she looked just like an angel.

I just stared up at her as she floated there above me. At one point I actually reached up, thinking that I would be able to touch her. As I reached, her smile grew bigger, and then she slowly floated up towards the ceiling. Once she got to the ceiling, she continued floating upward until eventually she was out of sight. I looked at my wife, trying to figure out how I was going to bring up the fact that there was a strange woman in our bedroom, but she was still asleep. I looked at the clock and saw that only one minute had passed. I got an overwhelming feeling that everything was going to be fine. I closed my eyes, and within a few minutes, I was asleep. This vision visited me several times. For a while, I was seeing her at least once a week.

Did this "angel" visit me just to put me at ease so I could sleep? Perhaps she was just a product of my overactive imagination. I don't know for sure and most likely will never know. What I do know is that her visit that night not only eased me into a nice, refreshing sleep, but it also wasn't to be my last visit from something strange. Sometimes I saw other things that I can't really explain; some were weird, some were downright scary.

One of the strangest things I saw appeared a couple nights after I told my wife what I was going through on nights when I couldn't sleep. The things I was seeing seemed so real that part of me thought for sure Heather would be able to see them too. As I was lying in bed with my eyes closed, I got the feeling again that I if I opened my eyes, I would see something. Sure enough, I opened my eyes to find a man floating above me. He wore a black and white striped outfit like the ones convicts wore on old TV shows.

I yelled for Heather to wake up and told her to look toward the ceiling, where the man in the prison garb was floating. I was excited because he was going away and I wanted her to see him before he disappeared. She said she couldn't see anything, even though I could still see him. I was really upset because I wanted proof that it wasn't just me being crazy. I wanted us to be crazy together! In sickness and in health, in sound and crazy minds, we are supposed to stick together. Unfortunately, since she didn't see it, I felt like I was the only crazy one. One night, I even saw our dog, Kolby Jack, visit us. Kolby had passed away months before, but on this night he returned. As I was lying in bed watching TV, I saw him float over the bed. I watched him move from Heather's side of the bed to my side. He then floated through the wall and was gone. Oddly enough, the place where he went through the wall is directly over where his body is buried. We buried him below our bedroom window so he would always be near us.

For the next several years, I would see things every once in a while. Sometimes it would be my angel, sometimes it would be other characters. On one occasion I saw something that I can only describe as a gargoyle. That one really got to me because I thought it was some kind of bad omen. I'm still here, though, so all's good on that front. The gargoyle was perched on the side of the bedroom wall, looking down at me. He wasn't floating as the others had been. Any time I've seen a gargoyle, they've always been perched on buildings, so this must have been the only way my mind knew how to convey this image to me. I could clearly make out his red eyes, and his claws, but I couldn't tell if he was alive or carved from stone. He didn't move, at any rate. I just closed my eyes and when I reopened them, he was gone.

One of the other strange things I saw appeared only once. I am glad for that because it terrified me more than the gargoyle did. As I was lying in bed trying to sleep, I heard a noise coming from above me. It sounded like a squirrel or some other animal was running around in our attic. I was lying on my side this time and I rolled over to my back. When I looked up, there appeared to be three figures floating above the bed. They looked like people with no facial features. For some reason, they reminded me of death. I thought it was a sign that something bad was going to happen. As with the gargoyle vision, I closed my eyes tightly. When I reopened them, the figures were gone.

I had a lot of trouble falling asleep after that. I know I was awake for at least the next three hours. I was concerned that if I fell asleep I wasn't going to wake up. I honestly felt that these three individuals were there to take me away and I wasn't ready to go. I can tell you that it was going to take all three of them to drag me from my family. After hours of not falling asleep, I had a calm feeling come over me. It was warm, gentle and comforting. I opened my eyes, and sure enough, there was my angel. She smiled at me, I smiled at her and asleep I went.

That was the last time I remember ever seeing something frightening when I was trying to fall asleep. I wondered if the angel was visiting me periodically to protect me from the three sinister figures that I saw that night. All I can say is, she did her job, and helped me get my rest in the process.

Now we come to the main reason I brought these night visitors up. Early on, when I was first experiencing visions, I was visited by the head of a lion. It was humongous and was right in front of my face. It looked at me as if we knew each other. I looked at it for a bit and then rolled over and fell asleep. Shortly after I started having these visions, we did the investigation at the cemetery. I really wanted to know what these things meant and why they were visiting me. Up to that point, I had only seen the angel and the lion.

I decided to ask our psychic lady if she could explain it to me. I explained that I have trouble sleeping and one night, I was visited by an angel, and then I was able to sleep. She said that what appears to be an angel may be a deceased family member who is trying to help me and is worried about me. Then she asked if I ever saw an animal. I told her I had been visited by a lion. She said that was a good sign. She said everyone has spirit guides that help them through life. These spirit guides can be human or animals. She said a lion spirit guide represents courage. She went on to say that I probably had gone through a lot in life and had faced a lot of adversity. The reason I made it through all of it was because my lion was with me the whole time to help me face things bravely and confidently.

Regardless of whether she was blowing smoke up my you-know-what, it made me feel really good. I started thinking, *yeah, I have been through a lot*, but that could apply to almost anyone. Everyone has problems; everyone faces challenges in their lives. I tried to push those thoughts out of my head and just appreciate the fact that what she said made me feel better about things. In the end, I think that's what we all want when we talk to psychics. We want to know everything is going to be fine. We want to know that our departed loved ones are still with us, keeping an eye on us to protect us from harm. Psychics, even those who aren't entirely on the up and up, can offer people that sense of closure. So for that, they have some value. But I still am, and will probably always be, just a bit skeptical.

9. Anna's Ghost

In the spring of 1962, tragedy struck the small southern Illinois town of Mascoutah. Early one April morning, a 79-year-old woman named Anna was burning trash in her yard when her dress accidentally caught fire. Anna ran into her basement, struggling to remove the burning garment. About ten minutes later, a mail carrier heard her screams. He ran around the back of the house and into the basement, where he found Anna engulfed in flames. An ambulance was called and she was taken to a local hospital, where she died. Eerily, it was reported in her obituary that all of her body was removed from her home, with the exception of her legs. The obituary failed to mention what became of the legs. I'd have to assume that the fire did so much damage that there just wasn't anything left of them.

Polaroid photo of Anna's house

Shortly after Anna's death, a couple with three young children moved into the home. At first, they all shared a bedroom on the lower level. It didn't take long for Anna to welcome her new guests. One of the children, a boy whom I'll call Jason, was awakened late one night. He sat up in bed and found that his parents were standing in the doorway, looking towards the staircase leading to the second floor. Jason could see that they were clearly bothered by something, he just didn't know what. He sat there rubbing the sleep from his eyes and trying to figure out what his parents were doing. Just then, he heard footsteps walking across the floor above them.

The footsteps went back and forth. It sounded like multiple people were moving around up there. The sounds continued for a long time as the puzzled new homeowners tried to figure out what it could be that they were hearing.

After Jason's mother made it clear that she wasn't going to going to be the one to go and see what was happening, his father went to investigate. He could find nothing wrong upstairs. The footsteps stopped. The closets, the windows, all the rooms, the nooks, the crannies, everything was normal.

The sound of footsteps continued nightly for weeks. The father would always get out of bed to check, but would never be able to find anything. Were the mysterious noises just the house settling, or was the house haunted? It would take a bit more activity before the family found out.

On another occasion, Jason woke up at night to see something standing in the bedroom doorway. It looked female, and initially he thought it was either his mom or his sister. As he looked closer, he realized it wasn't a person at all, but a dress hovering in the doorway. There was no face, no body – just a dress. He blinked his eyes, hoping it would go away, but the dress continued to hang there. Finally, he pulled the sheets up over his head. When he woke up the next morning, the dress was gone.

He tried to think of an explanation for what he had seen. The only thing he could come up with was that maybe his grandmother came to visit and had stood in the doorway to check on him. He asked his mother if his grandma had been there. As can probably guess, the answer was no.

As Jason grew older, he and his brother, whom I'll call Thomas, moved into one of the upstairs bedrooms. By this time, they were accustomed to the occasional nighttime noises. They were no longer terrified. They accepted the fact that their house was haunted. Things happened consistently the entire time they lived in the home. Sounds of someone walking throughout the rooms, sounds of furniture being moved around, and disembodied voices were all commonplace.

Eventually, two more siblings were born. As the family grew, the paranormal activity started to pick up.

The father started working swing shifts. Work was tough, but when you have five kids, it was also a way to get away from things. One night, when the youngest son was two years old, the father came home from work around midnight. The youngest son was still up, and the two of them sat on the couch and watched some late-night TV together.

As they sat there engrossed in the television show, a ghost made its appearance. This time, the ghost was a child. Both father and son saw a young boy pass through the middle of the room. He made his way across the room and passed through a wall, paying no attention to the people on the couch.

Instances where ghosts go about their business without appearing to be aware of any living people present are called residual hauntings. The ghost has no consciousness; it is merely an image that repeats an activity the same way over and over again. The wall that the ghost boy walked through may have been a doorway in years past. Or maybe the boy inhabited a different structure that was on the site before the house was built.

In any event, seeing a ghost walk through a wall startled the father. He thought his eyes were playing tricks on him. He was tired; the room was dark and the TV was on. All of those things could have made him imagine he saw the boy. It was at that point that his son asked, "Who was that little boy?" This same boy was spotted another time running in circles around the kitchen table.

Odd things continued to happen throughout the years. When Jason was twelve, he had another encounter. He was in bed asleep when he woke up to find a white, hooped dress standing at the foot of the bed. Like the first dress that he saw hovering the doorway, this one had no body inside it. Jason kept opening and closing his eyes, trying to make it go away, but the dress stayed there. Eventually, the covers went up over his head and remained that way until morning.

A year after that, Jason and Thomas were home alone one afternoon. They were both upstairs when they heard someone walking downstairs. The footsteps sounded leisurely, as if someone was just pacing aimlessly around. Initially the boys thought it was one of their parents or their siblings, but they were all out and were not supposed to return home for a long time.

As they continued to listen, without warning, all hell broke loose. It sounded like someone was hitting the walls as hard as they could. There were sounds of doors slamming, someone jumping violently up and down, and things breaking. Jason and Thomas thought someone had broken in and was wrecking the place. They dove under the bed and decided to wait it out. Shortly after taking their positions, they decided that under the bed is probably one of the worst hiding places if you are ever scared out of your mind. My initial visions of hiding under a bed usually bring to mind scenes from horror movies that I've seen. Being dragged out by the feet as you kick and scream is clearly not a good way to go. Ever seen *Poltergeist*? The thought of having a crazed intruder jump on the bed and start sticking a tire iron through the mattress, inches from your face, is also a little unsettling. No matter how they looked at it, Jason and Thomas needed a new plan.

They crawled out from under the bed and each of them grabbed a baseball bat. They cautiously made their way to the stairs leading down to the first floor. At this point, about twenty minutes had passed since the ruckus stopped. Just as they were about to descend the stairs, they heard a knock at the front door. It was their buddy, coming to see what they were up to. They told him to come in and come upstairs. That way, they reasoned, if anyone was hiding inside the house, their unsuspecting friend would be used as live bait to lure them out.

The friend responded that the screen door was locked and he couldn't get in. They called out to him to go around to the back door. He found that door was locked, as well. When Jason and Thomas checked, both screen doors were indeed locked. The weird thing was they were both locked from the inside with an eyehook latch. Whatever had been making the commotion couldn't have gotten in with both doors locked. It also couldn't have left and locked the doors behind it. So maybe it was still in the house with them...

They never found anyone (or anything, for that matter) inside the house that day. In fact, despite all the noise the boys heard, there was no mess. Surely, with all the commotion there would be open doors and cabinets, broken picture frames on the floor, and things strewn about, but nothing was out of place.

The last unusual experience that Jason told me about happened when his parents went away on an overnight trip to a cabin, leaving the kids home by themselves. Of course, they had to take advantage of the situation by throwing a party. The next morning, their father came home and picked them up to take them to the cabin. Jason and Thomas left one of their friends at the house with strict instructions to have the place cleaned up by the time they got home.

After the friend finished cleaning up the debris from the party, he made his way out to the front porch to sit and relax. As he sat there, he kept hearing noises coming from inside the house. It sounded as if kids were running up and down the stairs. They were laughing, giggling, and just having a grand old time. Curious to find out what was going on, he got up and went back inside.

This photo shows the door leading to the cellar. The house may also be haunted by the spirit of the chicken seen roasting on the grill in this photo. The chicken spirit is just a personal theory.

To his surprise, there was no one there. Everything was the way he left it. He just shrugged it off and went back to the porch. He wasn't out there very long when he heard voices coming through the bedroom window next to the porch. With that, he reached inside the front door, turned the latch, and left. Jason told me it was quite some time before his friend was willing to return to the house.

The family moved out of the house in 1977. There have been other owners since then, but from what I can tell, the haunting has slowly faded away. From what I hear, families that have lived there over the past three decades have experienced no ghostly activity at all.

Something strange went on in the house after Anna died from the horrible burns she received in the backyard. Were the footsteps hers as she roamed around her former house? Was the dress that Jason saw hanging in his doorway the one that Anna wore when she was involved in that tragic incident? Were the crashing sounds that Jason and Thomas heard the sounds of Anna flailing in agony as she was being burned alive? And what about the ghost boy who walked through the wall, or the children's voices that Jason's friend heard? Since the hauntings have stopped, we may never know. As with most paranormal cases, there may be more questions than answers when it comes to what went on inside Anna's house.

10. Black Cat Spotted in Mascoutah

Cryptozoology involves the search for animals whose existence has not been proven. This includes looking for living examples of animals that are considered extinct, such as dinosaurs and Tasmanian tigers; animals whose existence lacks physical evidence but which appear in myths and legends, such as Bigfoot and Chupacabra, and wild animals that are sighted far outside their normal geographic ranges, such as phantom cats (also known as Alien Big Cats).

Strange animals have been spotted all over the country by various people, some who are labeled crazy and some who are thought of as upstanding pillars of the community. Some claim to have seen Bigfoot or lake monsters, while some reported seeing large cats, wolves, etc.

Years ago, I saw a strange animal during one of our events at History & Hauntings Book Company in Alton. Someone spotted it from the front of the store and pandemonium ensued. While the ghost enthusiasts were chasing after it, I stood by and watched from the safety of the front porch, laughing as the scene played itself out. It turns out the bizarre-looking animal was just a dog/coyote with a bad case of mange.

That's not to say that some truly weird creatures don't appear in unexpected places. I recently spoke with former Mascoutah resident John Foster about an encounter he had with a mysterious animal. It was one of those out-of-place things that you can't believe when you see it. The interesting part of this story is that it comes from a credible witness who wasn't alone when the event took place.

Mysterious Alton animal.. not so mysterious

Foster was a full-time patrolman with the Mascoutah Police Department from 1972 to 1975. It was during that time that he had an extraordinary experience that he has never forgotten. Forty years later, he is still able to remember it as if it were yesterday. Some details have left his mind, such as the time of year, although he thinks it was in the spring or summer. However, he vividly remembers what he saw.

When this event occurred, the Mascoutah Police Department had only a few police cars. One was an old, white Chevrolet that probably rolled off the assembly line in the mid-sixties; one was a 1972 Ford LTD and the other was a 1974 Plymouth. Foster can't stay for sure which car he was riding in on the night in question, but it was one of those three. He remembers that he was riding with another patrolman on the 8 p.m. to 4 a.m. shift.

Foster was in the passenger seat and his partner was behind the wheel. It was around 2 a.m. when they drove out to the city cemetery on Lake Road.

It was part of the regular patrol to drive through the cemetery and ensure that the chapel and the garage were secure. In those years, there were no houses or apartments across from the cemetery. The closest house was probably the Etling farm, off the northeast corner of Harnett Street and Lake Road. The high school was across the fields to the south, the Silver Creek bottoms were to the west, and farm fields were to the north and east. It was a quiet and isolated place.

The hour was late and the air was clear. Foster and his partner were talking casually as they drove north out to the cemetery on Lake Road. Entering the cemetery from the south, they drove into the main entrance and followed the road to the right that led north and then widened as it passed between the chapel on the east and grave markers to the west. The road intersected with an east-to-west access road on the north side of the cemetery's equipment garage. At that point, they would be making a 90-degree turn to the left, which would lead them down the length of the cemetery. But before they could make the turn, they would witness something that has stayed burned into John Foster's memory to this day.

As they drove up to the old chapel and its west side came into view, something next to the building caught his eye. He turned his attention toward this spot, a small grassy area along the foundation of the building, and saw a large, black figure with menacing eyes that shone in the glare of the patrol car's headlights. Instantly, the owner of the eyes turned and sprang across the road, disappearing among the tombstones to the left. The animal took no more than three bounds to cross a thirty-foot-wide area before disappearing into the darkness.

Foster's partner turned on the spotlight to try and locate the animal, but they never saw it again. They drove throughout the cemetery, slowly scanning everywhere with the spotlight, but they never caught another glimpse of it. After searching for what seemed like hours, they drove back to the chapel and got out to look around. They could find nothing around the chapel where they first saw the animal. Neither was there any trace of it in the road or by the tombstones. Despite the fact that the animal had been large and had taken several mighty leaps as it bounded away, it left no paw prints.

The two men discussed what they had seen. They agreed that it had been coal black, had a short snout and small ears, a long slender tail and was muscular and sleek. In other words, it was a black cat, but it had been huge, like a panther. They found this hard to believe, but they had seen it with their own eyes. By Foster's calculation, the cat had been approximately two feet high and maybe three to four feet long, not including the tail, which looked to be two or three feet long. From head to tail it was approximately five to seven feet in length. Not your average field cat, by any means.

They tried to figure out what it could have been. Did its eyes glow red? Did they see its white teeth gleaming in the moonlight? Was it really a cat or could it have been a dog? They knew what they thought it was, but they had a difficult time coming to terms with that they knew.

A dog would not have leaped as this animal had done. Dogs run; this thing had bounded like a cat does. It had a long, slim tail that did not taper toward the end. The tail also appeared to be as long as its entire body length, much like a cat's. It had the short face of a cat and small ears. For sure, this had been a cat of some kind, and a very large one at that. Foster and his partner talked about the mystery animal for the rest of the shift. They searched the cemetery several more times after that unsettling evening, but they never saw anything remotely like the animal again.

Foster and his partner made a pact not to say anything about what they had seen. They didn't think anyone would believe them, and they didn't want to be ridiculed. I am sure that their desire for secrecy had a lot to do with the fact that they didn't relish the idea of filing a report on what they had witnessed. A report like that would involve a lot of explaining, and possibly a psychiatric evaluation.

Shortly after this sighting, Foster was on alone on patrol duty around midnight when he got a radio call from the operator of the town water plant. The plant operator reported that he thought he heard a woman's scream coming from the direction of the creek bottoms. The water plant at that time was located by the reservoir on the west end of town by Silver Creek.

Foster drove west on Route 177 to the creek bottoms and listened, but heard nothing. He started thinking about the black cat. He wondered uneasily if it had attacked someone. He decided to drive to the cemetery and have a look around. Once again, there was no sign of the cat.

Next, Foster drove to an area directly behind the high school, between the cemetery and the water plant. He searched with his spotlight, but saw and heard nothing. There was a baseball diamond behind the school, and under the stands were several doors, one of which was open. Foster grabbed his flashlight and entered the doorway, which led to an equipment room and a restroom with a single stall. The stall door was closed, so Foster cautiously pushed it open. Thoughts of the black cat were still in his mind. He wondered nervously if it could be in there, drinking out of the toilet. The worst-case scenario was that a woman had been taken into the room and murdered. Her body could be in the stall, or maybe the murderer was hiding in there.

Foster slowly pushed the door open with his pistol in hand. As the door swung open, he beheld a human form seated on the toilet. Foster jumped at the sight. It was several very tense seconds before he realized the figure was a tackling dummy wearing a football helmet. It had obviously been put there by high school kids as a prank to scare some unsuspecting person. They would probably have been delighted if they had known that their victim would be a police officer.

After checking the rest of the area, Foster drove to the water plant and talked to the operator. They concluded that the screaming was probably an owl or a bobcat. After a few days, Foster found the incident humorous, but he has always wondered just it was that the water plant operator heard that night.

Foster kept his end of the bargain for years. With the exception of his wife, he never told anyone about the black cat he and his partner saw that night. Then one day, he was reading a book about strange animal sightings. There was a chapter on huge black cats, including some that were seen in Missouri and Illinois. He wondered if the animal in the cemetery could have been one of these. He has never heard of any similar reports in the Mascoutah area, nor have I. But if John Foster kept his sighting a secret for all these years, then maybe there are others who saw the cat, but were reluctant to say anything. Or maybe the last person to see it was the woman whose screams were heard that night near the water plant, as she met a horrible end. (Insert creepy laughter here.)

11. Railroad Crossover

Growing up in Belleville, Illinois, I heard a lot of stories about places you could go to get the you-know-what scared out of you. Stories about haunted cemeteries, the Seven Gates of Hell, haunted houses, witches' graves, Indian ghosts and more, were told by people who either claimed to have personal experience with these places or who knew someone whose cousin dated someone whose best friend worked with a guy… Well, you get the picture. Out of all the places I had heard about, the one that intrigued me the most as a kid was the Haunted Railroad Tracks.

The reason why the railroad tracks are supposed to be haunted varies depending on whom you talk to. I have heard a number of stories about these tracks through the years. All of them have the same ending as far as a tragedy happening. In most cases, the stories involve an albino, although they differ as to whether it was a child or an adult.

Intersection of Rentchler Road and Rentchler Station

The most common story that I heard growing up was that there was an albino boy who was ridiculed by the other kids in school. One day, some kids were chasing him on the way home from school when he ran across the railroad tracks and was hit by a passing train.

Another variation of the story was that an epidemic passed through the area and devastated the local population. An albino who had moved there shortly before the epidemic was blamed for bringing the disease with him. In revenge, the locals tied him to the tracks, and well, you know the rest.

Yet another version of the story involves a group of kids who took the family horse and wagon for a joyride one night. The wagon got stuck on the tracks and was struck by a speeding train, killing all the children. No mention was made of the horse's fate. Out of all the stories, this was the one that I have heard the least, so I think it can be written off as pre-automobile era cautionary tale about the danger of joyriding.

The tracks used to run above this drainage pipe, on the left side of the road.

The railroad tracks were located off Highway 177, between Belleville and Mascoutah. Even though I heard about them as a kid, I didn't get the opportunity to go there until I was in my twenties. My wife, who is from Mascoutah, knew all about them and had been there before.   So one night, we decided to go out there. The group consisted of my lovely wife, her cousin Johnny, our best friend, Chasidy, and myself. We all piled into my wife's Chevy Beretta and set off to have what we hoped would be an adventure.

What we discovered made me believe that the location could very possibly be haunted. The railroad tracks have been removed, but you can tell where they were used to be. To the east and west, you can see the straight clearing where the tracks used to run through the fields and trees.

The concept behind the story is that the ghost of whoever it was who died on the tracks will push on the rear bumper of cars parked near where the tracks used to be. One theory is that the ghost is trying to help move the cars over the tracks and out of the way of oncoming trains. Another theory (one much darker, which I prefer because it makes the story creepier) is that the ghost is attempting to push cars onto the tracks in the hope that a train will hit them.

Either way, the ghost doesn't seem to have noticed that the tracks are no longer there. This doesn't speak very well for its intelligence.

People sometimes put flour or baking soda on the trunks or bumpers of their cars prior to rolling over the place where the tracks used to be. Once across, fingerprints will be visible, as if made by the hands of the spirit that pushed the car.

To experience the phenomenon of being "helped" across the tracks, you have to drive over the place where the tracks were and stop your car. Or, you can drive over where the tracks were, turn around, and then stop in front of the hill. Then all you do is put the car in neutral and wait. I suggest facing the place where the tracks used to be, so you don't have to navigate the terrain while rolling backwards. There have been times when people decided to roll backwards, only to end up off the road because they got confused going in reverse. It's also a good idea to go forward in case you need to make a quick getaway. That way, you are already facing in the right direction.

Once you are in position, and the car is in neutral, you will be sitting still for what seems like forever. You will start to feel pretty freaked out by the surrounding trees and vast fields. After a while, you'll feel your car start to move. It'll start off moving slowly, and then it will build up speed until you'll be up and over the mound that the tracks used to rest on. Sometimes, prior to the car moving, you'll feel a bump as if someone is giving you are a push. Once you get over the mound, remember to hit the brakes. Oh yeah, and unlike Troy Taylor, don't get out of your car to watch what happens if there's nobody at the wheel! Troy had to run after his car and jump in as it rolled along with no one steering it.

There doesn't seem to be a dip in the road that would cause cars to roll forward. Even if there was a hill to roll down and build up speed, it doesn't seem like you could get up enough speed to go over the mound. You could have your car right in front of the upward mound, and you would still roll over it. So you have to throw out the theory of gravity rolling you forward. It could be an optical illusion; it's hard to say. It's a strange world we live in, that's about the only thing I can say for sure.

The night that we went out there, it was an October evening and we were in the mood for an adventure. The temperature was cool, it was a bit windy, and it was a nice clear night. It was a perfect night for going to a haunted location to see if the spirits were going to come out and play. Before we got to the tracks, we applied flour to the trunk of our car in the hope of seeing the ghostly fingerprints. We spread the flour all over the bumper, as well. If it was the ghost of a child doing the pushing, I figured he would probably push on the bumper instead of on the trunk. (See, I'm always thinking.) Then we got back in the car and discussed how we wanted to get into position for this adventure.

107

Haunted railroad tracks dead ahead

We were the only ones out there, so we had the first pole spot. I felt better about rolling forward instead of in reverse. That way, if I had to take off in a hurry, I'd be aiming in the right direction. If you roll backwards, there's a dead end straight ahead of you. Once you get over the place where the tracks once were, you'll have the big curve in the road to deal with if you're moving backwards. So, we drove over the spot, turned around, and stopped the car about twenty feet in front of the mound. I shifted into neutral. Then we sat still and waited.

It only took a few moments before we started to slowly roll. As we got closer to the mound, we picked up quite a bit of speed. My hands were gripping the steering wheel so tightly at this point that my knuckles turned white. Once we were up and over, I hit the brakes and we stopped. We were all kind of blown away by the event. We just sat there for a minute, wondering if it really happened. I remember all of us just kind of looking at each other, waiting for someone to say something. Of course, no one did. At this point my wife and I decided to get out and check for fingerprints on the back of the car. We were just over the hill, so when we got out to have a

108

look, we were only standing about ten feet from the place where the tracks used to be. I was kind of getting nervous because my back was to it. If the ghosts of the joyriding farm kids (for some reason I thought of them, instead of the albino boy or the albino man) could push you across the tracks in a car, would it be possible for them to drag you back across them, car or no car? I was really surprised at what happened next because it wasn't what I expected.

I am sure at this point you are probably thinking that there were fingerprints on the trunk of our car. And you are right, we did find fingerprints, but that's not the cool thing that happened; we'll get to that in a moment. In our case, I think the fingerprints can be explained. If you picture a car covered with flour, and someone were to put their fingertips into the flour, you would see the fingerprints surrounded by the untouched flour. The back of our bumper looked a lot different. It looked like someone dipped his hand in flour and then touched the car with his fingertips. It was breezy that night. I think at some point, we had touched the trunk and bumper with our hands. Then, when we poured the flour on it, and the wind started to blow, the flour stuck to where we had touched the car. The moisture from our fingers is probably what made the flour stick in the shape of fingerprints. The rest of the flour was gone, blown right off the car. It could have been the ghostly hands of a helpful spirit or it could have been the hands of some ghost enthusiasts who didn't plan for a windy evening. So here's a word of advice: If you do the flour trick, make sure you thoroughly clean your car first. Secondly, make sure it's a calm night with no wind or rain. Lastly, don't apply the flour until right before getting ready to do the experiment.

Although the flour experiment was inconclusive, something else happened that evening that made us think there was something to the story about the tracks being haunted. When Heather and I got out of the car to check on the flour, we both heard noises coming from the cornfield. I heard it right away, but I didn't say anything.

I looked at Heather and saw he lift her head and look towards the field. I asked her if she heard something and she said she did. We both heard the sounds of children laughing coming from the field. The laughter was very clear and sounded like it was right next to us. It sent shivers up and down my spine. We figured we'd had enough for the night and got back in the car and headed home.

Since I always try to find a rational explanation for things, my initial thought was that maybe the sound traveled from one of the neighboring houses. The problem with this theory is that it's in the middle of nowhere, and houses are few and far between. The other issue is that it was about 11:30 at night. It doesn't seem likely that kids would be out playing that late. What was eerie about the voices was that it sounded to me like the kids were laughing and singing something that sounded like "Ring around the Rosie." I know when I was a kid, and I was out that late at night, I wouldn't be singing anything like that. I would have been making up my own song about how I was going to get in trouble if my parents knew I was out.

I had been talking to several people, trying to acquire more stories for my readers. At the time I was writing this book, I was doing a promotion with a local theater for a special October re-release of *Ghostbusters*. I was set up in the lobby, telling ghost stories, selling books, listening to stories, all that good stuff. I was also writing some of this book while I was there. As people came up to me, I asked them if they had ever been to the haunted railroad tracks. Some had, some hadn't. Some said they were too scared, and some planned on going soon. I also had the following cool story told to me, so I figured I'd share it with you.

This is one of those stories told to me by a friend of the person who had the experience. Usually I only like to include first-hand accounts, but as you'll soon see, I had to include this one. A young lady told me about her friend who went out to the tracks one night around 9:30. He did the car trick, and it worked, but he also decided to do a little more investigating on foot. He started to walk west along the area where the tracks once lay. It was gradually getting darker the farther he got into the wooded area. All of a sudden, he started hearing kids laughing and singing. It sounded as if they were right behind him. At first, he didn't want to turn around to look, but he was going to have to turn around eventually, because that was the way he needed to go if he was going to get back to his car. As was getting ready to turn around, he realized that he couldn't move.

At this point, he started really getting frightened. The hair was standing up on his neck. The kids' voices were crystal clear. This went on for about a minute, and then just as quickly as it started, the laughter and singing ended and he was able to move again. When he turned around, he saw nothing but darkness and trees behind and around him.

He debated about going home at this point, but he wanted to explore the area just a little bit more. He began to walk on a bit farther. As he progressed down the lane, all of a sudden he heard a train whistle coming from out of nowhere. It was very loud and sounded as if it was all around him, engulfing him. It actually made his ears ring and his head hurt because it was so loud. Even though the tracks were gone, his first instinct was to see which direction the train was coming from. He looked off in the distance and saw what looked like a white light coming towards him. Remember, the railroad tracks are no longer there, yet he could hear a train and see its light. He watched it for about a minute, and then just like the children's voices, it was gone. At this point, he decided that his evening would be better spent at home, and he headed back to his car.

I was excited to hear this story because it involved someone else who reported hearing kids laughing, just like my wife and I did. I like hearing about multiple people having the same experience at different times, and without any knowledge of others having had the experience. Something like that adds a whole new level of substantiation to reports of paranormal activity.

Some folks swear this area is haunted. Others insist that a combination of gravity and momentum pulls vehicles up and over the tracks. As far as my opinion goes, it's still up in the air. I've been there, I've experienced the phenomenon, but I don't have all the answers. Unfortunately, it's a dead end road, and there are people who live out there. I am sure they get annoyed with thrill seekers constantly coming down the road late at night. So if you do plan on going, remember that the living can be just as scary as the dead. They can be even scarier when they are protecting their property, so keep that in mind and be respectful if you're ever in the vicinity and decide to go out there.

12. Hospitals: Some Patients Stay Longer to Get Their Money's Worth

Since I know several people who work in hospitals and other health care facilities, I thought it would make for an interesting chapter to report on some of the spirits that these buildings hold. Of course in doing so, I have to protect the anonymity of those who spoke with me about their ghostly experiences. I also don't want to identify the facilities by name because they are still in operation.

Think about all the suffering and tragedies that have occurred at health care facilities. How could they not have some kind of paranormal activity? Most of the haunted hospitals that you hear about on television or in books are no treating patients. Places like Waverly Hills Sanatorium in Louisville, Kentucky, come to mind immediately. Yes, Waverly Hills is very haunted, and I have had my share of personal experiences there. You'll have to read my first book, *The Lighter Side of Darkness,* to hear those stories. This time, I want to delve into some stories from places that are still in operation. You can go there, and you don't need to pay for a tour or arrange for a private investigation. These hospitals are the ones where, with a little luck, you can get hurt and stay the night there for free. Well, not really for free, in fact, it will probably be quite expensive. Unless you have insurance, that is. But even then, you still have to pay a deductible. I'm rambling, but I am sure you get the point, so I'll move on.

Patients died in droves at Waverly Hills during the height of the tuberculosis epidemic, but modern hospitals experience their share of deaths, too. So why wouldn't they be haunted? Since people are still working in these places, it greatly increases the chances of someone witnessing any ghostly happenings. In most cases, these witnesses are very intelligent, analytical health care professionals who have serious work to do, and aren't there with the intent of finding ghosts. I think stories coming from within the walls of a place that still has employees scurrying about, and patients coming in and out, can be a hotbed for some wonderfully entertaining ghost stories. These are the kinds of hospitals that I am interested in.

I've interviewed several people who have either formerly worked, or continue to work at hospitals all over the St. Louis area. Strange things seem to happen at all hours, with no rhyme or reason to pinpoint why. In some cases, it could be caused by a tragic death. Maybe it was caused by someone who passed on and didn't realize that he was dead. It could be caused by a grieving family member who, like clockwork, used to visit the hospital at the same time every day. I think it could be all of the above. Here are some of the stories that were told to me by people who witnessed paranormal activity while they were just doing their jobs.

Betty's Stories

One eyewitness I spoke with is a registered nurse at a local hospital. I'll call her Betty. She came in to work after having had a couple of days off. Sadly, the day before, a patient passed away after a very long and painful bout with breast cancer. Betty was particularly close with the patient and had not found out that she had passed. As she approached the nurses' station, she saw the patient walking at the end of the hallway, going towards her room. Betty thought this was a little strange because normally this woman wouldn't be wandering around. When Betty made her way down to the patient's room, she found it was empty. All of the patient's things had been removed. Betty went back to the nurses' station, where another nurse told her that the breast cancer patient had died the day before. When Betty mentioned that she had just seen her walking at the end of the hall, the other nurse's face turned pale. It turns out that nurse had seen her too, but she thought she had imagined it. The woman was spotted a few more times over the next several days. Then she was no longer seen. Personally, I think she was just hanging around long enough to say her final goodbyes to those who had cared for her for so long.

On another occasion, Betty was in the hallway talking with another nurse. She was explaining how long a day it had been and how exhausted she was. She mentioned that her shoulders were aching from all the patients she had to lift that day. At that, she could feel someone standing behind her start to massage her shoulders. Her expression must have been blissful because the nurse she was talking to burst out laughing. Through her laughter, the nurse asked Betty, "What on Earth are you doing?"

Betty replied, "The shoulder massage feels incredible. It's just what I needed to get me through the rest of the day."

The other nurse asked, "Shoulder massage? What shoulder massage?"

"The one I am getting right now," Betty answered.

At this point, the nurse peered behind Betty and suggested that she turn around. To her amazement, there wasn't anyone behind her. Betty told me that it was very obvious that someone was rubbing her shoulders. She said it felt like a man because they were very strong hands. To this day, she has no idea who it was. It felt so soothing that even after knowing it was most likely a ghost masseuse, Betty said she would welcome him back anytime.

Her second experience with being touched by someone unseen involved a much more forward ghost. Betty was taking her allotted break one afternoon and found herself at the nurses' station talking with another nurse. She was leaning on the counter with her hands clasped in front of her. All of a sudden, she felt herself get goosed. She spun around to find out who did it, and of course there wasn't anyone there. The nurse she was talking to said there hadn't been anyone behind Betty when it happened.

Another of Betty's experiences involved a mysterious man in gray sweatpants. Betty has seen this gentleman all over the hospital. Although he appears to be real, she knows he isn't. She first came across him early on, when she first started working in the hospital. He was walking down one of the halls. Betty didn't recognize him, so she followed him to see where he was going. She saw him go into one of the rooms, but when she entered the room seconds later, he was nowhere to be seen. It was as if he had simply vanished. Betty relayed this experience to one of the other nurses, who said the man in the gray sweatpants is seen all the time around the hospital. She said she herself had seen him walking by the lounge earlier that same day.

Betty said the most frightening thing she has seen while at work was a gurney rolling down the hallway. She has seen it several times, usually just catching a glimpse of it out of the corner of her eye. She said she never sees anyone pushing the gurney; it always just seems to be moving by itself.

Gwen's Stories

Another nurse, whom I'll call Gwen, told me about something that happened regularly at a hospital where she used to work. One of the elevators seemed to have a mind of its own.   Throughout the night, the elevator will move from floor to floor without anyone operating it. Sometimes, if she watched the floor lights above the elevator, she would see one the lights jumping around from floor to floor. They had people stand at each floor in front of the elevator to see if anyone was pushing the buttons, but the elevator was always empty and there isn't anyone pushing the up or down button to call it to the floor.

This elevator activity was sometimes quite helpful. Often times, when Gwen would have her hands full with a tray of food, or laundry, the elevator doors would considerately open as she approached. Once she was inside, the floor button that she needed would already be lit up. The doors would close and the elevator would whisk her to her destination. This activity has been going on for years. The staff even has an affectionate name for the ghostly elevator operator. They call him Mr. C.

Gwen mentioned another experience she had that occurred in one of the patient's rooms. As she was working at the nurses' station, the call light went on for room 312. Gwen was the only one at the station at the time, so she made her way down the hall to see what was wrong. Much like Betty's story about the breast cancer patient, when she got to the room, it was empty. According to Gwen, this type of thing happened a lot in the hospital where she worked. They usually chalked it up to bad wiring causing the lights to come on, but the wiring was checked frequently, and nothing was ever found to be wrong with it.

Gwen said sometimes rooms show signs of having been occupied, even when there hadn't been anyone in them. Several times, she's gone into a room that had just been made ready for a new patient and found an imprint on the bed. It would sometimes appear as if someone had sat down on the bed. Other times, the imprint would be that of a person lying down. She's even experienced walking into a room, seeing the imprint, and then watching as it slowly smooths out, as if whoever had been sitting or lying there got up off the bed. She said it's a bit unnerving, but it comes with the territory and she's used to it.

Brenda's Stories

Brenda, yet another nurse I spoke to, told one of my favorite stories. She was working a midnight shift and the hospital was very quiet. As she was sitting at the nurses' station, something caught her eye. She got up and peered down the hall, where she saw one of the patients slowly walking. The strange thing was that this woman appeared to be completely oblivious when Brenda called her name. She just kept walking down the hall at a slow, steady pace. This is where the story gets strange. As the woman moved farther down the hall, a whitish glow starting to appear around her. Just as the woman turned a corner and was out of sight, an alarm from one of the patient monitors started to go off. Brenda ran down the hall to the room where the trouble was and found that the patient had passed. This was the same woman whom Brenda had just seen walking down the hall. Perhaps Brenda witnessed the woman's spirit moving on to the afterlife.

Brenda has also had her share of experiences with call lights going on for no reason. She spoke of one room in particular where the light will go off repeatedly throughout the day. This light does not come on if the room has a patient staying in it. It seems to only happen when the room is empty. Even though the staff knows this light only comes on when the room is empty, they also know that they can't ignore it. Perhaps the spirit that is making the light turn on is enjoying the attention it brings. The only way to make it stop lighting up is to actually take the time to go and check to make sure everything is okay in the room. The nurses will walk to the room, peek in, make sure all is well, and then move on. This is usually enough to satisfy the spirit, and they generally won't be bothered by the call light again until the room becomes occupied and then vacant again. Then, if the room is empty for too long, they'll have to complete the cycle again.

Orbs seem to be very common in health care facilities. All three of the nurses I spoke with described similar experiences. They all spoke of seeing balls of light moving from room to room during the evening hours. I asked if any would be seen during the day, but none of them could recall seeing them in daylight. It wouldn't be something they'd glimpse out of the corner of their eyes; the lights would appear straight ahead. They almost looked as if you could follow them, but all three nurses decided early on that there was no need to find out where the balls of light were going.

Raul's Stories

A fourth witness, whom I'll call Raul, told me about a very strange experience that occurred in the morgue at one of the hospitals where he worked in security. On one of his shifts, he was called down to the morgue to deal with a disturbance. A young woman had been brought to the hospital dead on arrival from a drug overdose and her body had been placed in the morgue. Her family had come to identify the body and were overcome with emotion. The girl's grandmother was taking it especially hard, and was causing quite a scene. They got her out of the morgue, but that only made things worse, because she was struggling to get back inside. This was the first bit of action Raul had that day, but it wasn't to be the last.

Later that day, one of the patients passed away and Raul had the duty of wheeling the body down to morgue. The first strange thing happened when he was pushing the body on a gurney towards the elevator doors. As he approached, the doors opened. He stood there, waiting for whoever was getting off the elevator to step out. When nobody did, he peeked in and saw the elevator was empty, so he pushed the gurney in. He was a bit confused by this because given the length of time he had waited for someone to step out of the elevator, the doors should have shut before he had a chance to get on. Instead, the doors had patiently remained open for him.

Once he got in the elevator, he went to push the lower level button for the morgue. Before he could reach it, the doors closed and the button lit up. It seemed as if somebody knew where he was going.

When he finally reached the entrance to the morgue, Raul noticed that the room where the bodies were kept was a bit overcrowded. He started to push the gurney in, and as he was doing so, he had to shift one of the other gurneys over to make some space. The gurney he was trying to scoot over held the body of the young woman that had come in earlier. As he moved the gurney, his hand brushed over the body bag. He could feel the corpse's foot press against his arm. He said he felt as if he received an electrical shock that ran straight through his body. At the same time, a cold gust of air blew from the direction of the young woman's corpse straight out the door. A stack of papers on a counter near the door were blown all over the floor by the rush of air. Needless to say, Raul finished his task and got out of there as quickly as possible.

Raul also mentioned an uneasy feeling that he gets on a couple of the hospital floors. He described it as a heaviness that totally overcomes him and weighs him down. He could be having the greatest day ever and be feeling on top of the world, and then he suddenly feels like he sprinted head-first into an emotional wall. His good mood evaporates and he feels terribly sad. Once he leaves the floor, the depressed mood goes away and he feels happy again.

He mentioned how he was involved in training a new security guard who asked him if he ever got a weird feeling on certain floors. When Raul asked which floors he was talking about, the trainee named the same ones where Raul experienced the emotional heaviness. Skeptics may say its coincidence, but according to Raul, he and the trainee are not the only ones who have sensed something unpleasant about these floors.

Mary Lou's Stories

Yet another witness, a woman whom I'll call Mary Lou, worked at one Illinois hospital for forty years. Mary Lou had quite an experience on the sixth floor of the hospital. Many years ago, a very angry elderly lady spent her last hours in room 610. She didn't have any family to visit her, so she must have been extremely lonely. Perhaps it's due to this state of loneliness that she didn't want anyone bothering her. Even when hospital employees tried to spend time with her, she made it very clear that she didn't want their company. She became very rude and hostile towards anyone who tried to talk to her.

Shortly after her death, strange things began to happen in Room 610. The room was said to be haunted and was usually avoided if at all possible. Like all the patient rooms, this one had a crucifix on the wall. Any time anyone would walk into Room 610, inexplicably the crucifix would fly off the wall and land halfway across the room. It was securely fastened to the wall with nails, so there's no reason why this would occur.

Other times, employees who entered the room would get the feeling that someone was standing either directly behind them or right next to them. This usually only happened when they were alone. The feeling was so unsettling that they would leave the room as soon as possible.

Mary Lou also spoke of a phantom patient who has been seen on numerous occasions wandering the sixth-floor halls. He wears a hospital gown, and although he seems to wander aimlessly, he always remains just out of reach of any staff members who try and follow him. The apparition will walk to the end of one of the hallways. Once there, he will turn and walk into a room. The problem is, he doesn't open the door first; he will just walk through it.

Her last story involves a nun who isn't really there. In this particular hospital, a lot of the nurses say they get the feeling that they are being watched. Most times, they will turn around and realize there is nobody there. Other times, they will see what appears to be the ghost of a nun. She holds a clipboard and wears a nun's habit. Those who have seen her describe her as being very stern-looking. She usually appears to be writing things down on her clipboard as she grimly peers at the employees. Perhaps in life she was the head nurse and kept a sharp eye out for nurses who were goofing off. The nurses always feel like they are being critiqued when she's around, so she must still be making sure all of them are working hard.

Sophia's Stories

One of my favorite stories involves yet another hospital in Illinois. I won't say which one it is, but with a little research, you might be able to figure it out. If you do, all I ask is that you remember that hospitals are in the business of caring for sick people, and they don't welcome prospective ghost hunters. Let the stories come to you, rather than you coming to them. That's how I feel when it comes to facilities like these that are still in operation. I've been fortunate that these stories were told to me. Once I spoke with someone who worked at a hospital, the floodgates opened and the stories started to flow out. One of the nurses I spoke to ended up mentioning it to another, who mentioned it to another, and before too long, I had an entire chapter about haunted hospitals.

This story involves a hospital parking garage. The garage isn't haunted because some tragic event occurred in it; the haunting is said to come from what happened on the site before the parking garage was built.

The story involves a building that was tied in with the hospital. It was thought to have either been an orphanage or some kind of childcare facility. Tragically, this building was destroyed in a fire in which some children may have lost their lives. I've done some research, but I haven't been able to verify any of this yet. Part of me wonders if this story was created to explain the odd things that have been reported in that area of the hospital's property. Often times, these stories are a way to cope with something that is difficult to understand. It's what we like to call "ghost lore."

In this case, the ghostly happenings involve children. Often times at night, when employees are leaving the hospital, they hear the sounds of children's voices, either inside the parking garage or as they approach the building. The children sound like they are running up and down, just having a grand old time. These sounds are heard late at night and very early in the morning, times when children would normally be in bed. There are never any adult voices present, just children. When the voices are heard, the witnesses usually try to locate the children to see if they are okay, or whether they need help finding their parents. Of course, no matter how hard they search, no children are ever found.

On several occasions, employees have actually seen a child standing among the cars. The child is always alone, and looks frightened and lost. Stories of people walking to their cars, seeing the child, and then going to approach him only to find that he is no longer there, are very common at this hospital. On some occasions, people have been driving through the garage when they saw a child standing in the middle of the exit lane. They'd put their car in park, get out of the vehicle, and the child would be gone.

Luke's Stories

Now, let me spin a tale involving one of my personal experiences at a hospital. I was in junior high when my grandma was hospitalized. Often times, when I went to visit her with my family, I would stay in her room for a bit, and then I would go hang out in the family lounge. My family had recently moved from the town where I had spent my whole life up to that point. I often used the payphone in the lounge to call the girls I used to date because calling them from my home phone was long distance.

During one of these times in the lounge, I ended up having a conversation with an older gentleman. I was sitting on the couch watching television when he walked in and sat down in one of the chairs. I was a bit shy as a kid, and it felt weird when older people tried to talk to me. At any rate, this man started talking to me, and although I didn't really want to talk to a stranger, it didn't take long to warm up to him. We were talking about the Cardinals, the television show that was on, and other things as well. He asked why I was at the hospital and I told him I was visiting my grandmother. He talked to me a bit about that and reassured me that all would be well with her.

We hit a spot in the conversation where there was awkward silence that was on the verge of becoming uncomfortable. At this, he put his hands on his knees and said he had more people to help and he must be going. He got up and started to make his way out of the lounge. He had to walk past me to get to the door. As soon as he passed me, I figured I'd better get back to my grandma's room. I turned around and the man was gone. I thought it was weird that he would be gone so quickly. I walked out of the lounge and looked both ways down the hall, but he was nowhere to be seen. To this day, I am not sure if he was real or not. In my opinion, I think he was a spirit that visited the hospital to not only be with the patients, but to be there for the families who needed him, as well.

This is how I looked in 8th grade, when I had the encounter with the old man in the hospital lounge. I figured I'd save one of the scariest photos for the end. Ah, the precious mullet! The laughs that come with this photo hopefully made your purchase of this book worth it.

I think a hospital is a perfect place to have one of those experiences with a ghost where you don't realize it was a ghost until afterwards. If you consider all the people milling about in a hospital, it's hard to discount the idea that one of them could be a ghost. Especially since most people at hospitals are there for a purpose. They stick to that purpose and often appear to be oblivious to what's occurring around them. Next time you are in a hospital, open your eyes and ears to what's around you. You may have an experience that you would have otherwise missed. As with my experience when my grandmother was in the hospital, open your heart too. The fact that this guy took time to talk to me, with my full-on mullet, Motley Crue t-shirt and ripped-up jeans, really meant a lot to me. It took my mind off things for a little while, and it made me feel better when he said everything was going to be okay.

13. Don't Forget the Night Light

Who would have thought that speaking at an event would open the door to learning about a wonderful family's ghostly tale? Well, it happened. In 2012, I spoke at the Espenschied Chapel in Mascoutah during the Halloween season. It was a night of ghost stories inside the chapel, followed by some great food, and ending with a leisurely stroll through the cemetery that surrounds the west side of the chapel. For those paying attention, this is the same building where the giant black cat was seen by the two police officers.

During the intermission, a lady named Michelle stopped by the table where I had my books and equipment set up. I was not at the table at that time, but my friend Chasidy was running things. Michelle mentioned that she had a lot of stories that she would love to share. She began to tell Chasidy about some of the strange things she's encountered through her life. I returned as was finishing up a few of her tales. She gave me her contact information so we could talk sometime. We kept in touch, but it wasn't until March 2013 that we were able to get together so I could hear her stories.

I brought Chasidy with me to Michelle's house one evening. I planned on only spending about an hour there because it wasn't going to be an investigation. Michelle told us that she had moved out of the home where the activity had occurred. Little did I know how much Michelle has moved around. She is in the Air Force and has bounced around quite a bit. It seems as though something may be making the moves along with her. In the following story, we'll move along with Michelle, from place to place, and meet some of her ghosts. Her adventures are many, so get comfortable. In the two-plus hours that we talked, we jumped around to different times in her life. I am going to try and organize the events so they flow in the correct order.

We will begin the story in 1994. Michelle was living in an apartment in Virginia at this time. She was dating a man whom we'll call Mike. The story is going to get a bit saucy for a moment, so bear with me. One evening, when Mike was visiting Michelle, they decided to take a shower together. Michelle was standing in front, near the shower head, and Mike was standing behind her. As Michelle was washing her hair, she saw the shower curtain slowly begin to open. Since she and Mike were the only ones there, she was thrown completely off guard.

As the curtain opened farther, Michelle saw a man staring in at her. She screamed and the curtain closed again. Mike, who had no clue as to what had just happened, asked her what was wrong. Michelle blurted out that a man had just peeked in at them. At that, Mike jumped out of the shower in all his naked glory and searched all over the apartment. There was no sign of anyone. The door was locked, the windows were closed; there was no way that someone could have gotten in. They quickly realized that whoever had peeked into the shower had simply vanished.

A couple of days later, Michelle heard sirens coming down her street. When she looked out the window, she saw police cars and an ambulance stopping a few doors down from her apartment. She went to see what was going on and found out that a man had passed away inside his home. According to the police, he had been dead for several days. When Michelle saw the photograph that ran with the man's obituary, she realized that it was the same man she had seen peeking into the shower. The strange thing was, he was already dead by the time she saw him.

This man wasn't the only spirit Michelle saw in the apartment. One evening, she came face to face with a little girl. She had on a beautiful white dress with a hoop skirt. The dress had a green ribbon at the waist that was tied into a big bow in the back. The girl's hair was long and dark, with long curls dangling along the side of her face.

Michelle even witnessed her dog playing with this spirit. She saw the spirit girl throw a ball down the hall, and the dog would get it and bring it back to her. Mike came home from work late one night and saw the dog playing in the hall. As Mike started to walk up the stairs, he saw the dog run past the top of the stairs as it followed a ball down the hallway. The dog then ran back with the ball in his mouth. Seconds later, it ran back past the stairs and retrieved the ball again. Mike thought Michelle must be playing fetch with the dog, but when he got to the hallway, there wasn't anyone there. Michelle was fast asleep in the bedroom.

After moving out of that apartment, Michelle moved to a duplex in Nebraska. She lived there from 1999 to 2005. While living in this home, she and Mike were married and started a family. They eventually had a daughter and a son. As the years passed, they encountered several strange things inside their home that they couldn't explain. Another family that lived in the other half of the duplex had their own ghost, which we will get to shortly. For now, let's start with the ghost that haunted Michelle's house.

One evening, while Michelle was pregnant with her son, she was taking a long, hot shower in the upstairs bathroom. Mike and their daughter Liv were both downstairs, working on the computer and watching television, respectively. The duplex wasn't very big and the upstairs bathroom wasn't much larger than a closet. It was so small that it was necessary to open and close the bathroom door repeatedly to be able to move around and take care of what needed to be done.

As Michelle got out of the shower and began to dry off, she opened the bathroom door and was surprised to see a young child run past down the hallway. Although the child looked boyish, it had long, light brown hair. Michelle thought it was her daughter. She called out to Liv but received no response. There was no sign of her daughter upstairs, so she went downstairs and asked

Mike where Liv was. Mike pointed to the couch, where Liv was watching TV. When Michelle told him she had just seen Liv run past the bathroom door, Mike said that was impossible because Liv had never left the couch. When Michelle described the child she had seen to him, Mike got chills. He had seen him, too, on numerous occasions.

The family got used to the spirit child. He was full of mischief but he would never do anything to intentionally scare them. Liv would sometimes play with him, and he acted like a normal, rambunctious little boy. They would chase each other and talk to each other. Often, when Liv would be sleeping, the boy would playfully pull the covers off of her.

On the other side of the duplex, it was a whole different story. It seemed as though the spirit that resided there was very malevolent. The family that lived there often spoke of seeing things, hearing noises throughout the night, and being physically tormented by a spirit. As Michelle put it, a very mean man haunted that side of the duplex.

Liv was at the other side of the house playing with the neighbors' son one afternoon. They were in the basement playing some games and coloring when Liv started to get scared. Just as they were about to head upstairs, one of the long fluorescent lights fell out of its ceiling fixture and crashed to the floor, right in front of the stairs. The bulb shattered and broken glass flew everywhere. The startled kids stopped in their tracks and looked down at the shards of glass. Just then, they heard a voice bellow, "Get out of my house!" At this, the kids ran right through the glass and raced upstairs as quickly as they could. Since they had been playing in their bare feet, Liv ended up getting a large piece of the glass lodged in her foot.

The angry spirit also terrorized the nursery. The mother, who was pregnant at the time, decided to decorate the room with Winnie the Pooh décor. Days after she put up a Pooh wallpaper border, she went into the nursery and found it had been torn down and ripped to shreds. They were never been able to explain how it happened.

The spirit also liked to play tricks on the family. The tricks weren't like the ones played by Michelle's ghost. These were the kind of tricks that people do to be hateful towards someone. Steve, the father, was legally blind. He had two dogs, both German shepherds. The dogs would often start barking and growling at something only they could see. They were very protective of their master, but sadly, they weren't always around.

Some of the tricks this spirit would play on Steve were very cruel. One time, Steve was working at his desk, he got up to get a Coke. Upon returning to the desk, he started to feel around for his chair, but it was gone. As he moved around, still unable to locate the chair, he put his hands down on the desk in frustration. When he did this, he bumped into the chair, which was now on top of his desk. Obviously, this was not where Steve had left it.

While working at his desk, Steve would set his drink down on the right side of the computer keyboard. That way, he would always know where it was since he was right-handed. His drink would sometimes move to the left side of the desk on its own. If he left it on the left side, it would be moved back to the right side. This would go on repeatedly. It seemed as if the spirit was doing this just to make things as difficult for Steve as possible.

One evening, Michelle was startled by police sirens in front of her house. She came out into the front yard to see what was going on. Her neighbors were outside. They said that they had just come home, and as they pulled up to the house, they saw the front door was open, all the window blinds were pulled up, and all the lights were on. They had been gone all day and thought for sure there was an intruder inside. The police checked everywhere but found no one. Nothing was missing, either. The family chalked it up to their malicious spirit.

Other examples of the activity in the neighbors' house included the kitchen chairs and other pieces of furniture being moved around. The final straw came when something pushed Steve down the stairs. He was not injured, but the family had had enough. After living in the house for about a year, they moved to Iowa to get away from the spirit.

The two spirits tended to stay on their separate sides of the duplex. Michelle's family got the good spirit, and Steve's family got the wicked one. They never seemed to cross from one side to the other except for one time. One of Michelle's best friends had passed away. This friend was like a big brother to Michelle, and she was honored when his family asked her to be a pallbearer. Michelle packed her bags and left for Virginia, leaving Mike at home with the kids.

The day after the funeral, Michelle got a phone call from Mike. He sounded terrified and demanded that she return home immediately. He said something was wrong with the house. Michelle had never heard him sound so scared. When she calmed him down, he told her what happened. He was lying in bed trying to fall asleep for the night. He had the lamp and television on because their two children were in bed with him. Mike was lying on his back, and he turned his head so he could check on the kids sleeping next to him. He turned back to look up at the ceiling and got the shock of his life.

The way Mike described it, it felt as if someone was sitting on his chest and pinning him down. He knew he was awake because he had looked at the children seconds before to make sure they were asleep. He could not move at all. It wasn't sleep paralysis, because he was alert and was able to feel his extremities moving; he just couldn't get up. He didn't want to wake the kids by screaming, because that would terrify them. He just lay there motionless. After several minutes, the weight finally left him and he was able to get up. At this point, he grabbed the phone and pleaded for Michelle to come home.

Michelle did a little research on the house. She contacted the police as well as the library and local historians. From what she found, there used to be a holding place for prisoners located where the house stood. The area they lived in was considered part of the Oregon Trail, so there is definitely a lot of history in that area. Years later, after Michelle's family moved away, the house was demolished. It was in very bad shape, with the kitchen floor held up by support jacks, so it was only a matter of time before it collapsed. They moved to another home in Nebraska, and they didn't have any paranormal experiences while living there.

After leaving Nebraska, Michelle and Mike moved to Scott Air Force Base in Illinois. They lived there from around January 2008 until 2012. Their duplex was located on a cul-de-sac. Although the family thought they were getting away from the spirits that haunted them in Nebraska, they would soon find out that they weren't alone in their new home. Not only was their home haunted, but several other homes in their cul-de-sac also had ghostly activity. We'll start with Michelle's stories, and then we'll cover a couple of her neighbors' stories.

The house on the cul-de-sac always had a strange feeling to it. When Michelle was laid up on disability, several friends and family members would visit her. Most of them commented that the house made them feel uneasy. Although they would visit, they would never stay the night. The house had such an uncomfortable, dark feeling that visitors preferred to go home rather than sleep there, regardless how late it was or how bad the weather may have been.

The family experienced a lot of problems with the house's electrical system. Michelle was always very conscientious about turning the lights off when no one was in a room, yet she would frequently find that the lights had been turned back on. The television would often turn itself on and off, as well.

Michelle liked to keep the doors open so she could keep an eye on her kids. Time after time, doors would slam shut by themselves as someone walked past. Other times, they would swing gradually shut.

One of Michelle's first experiences in the house happened one day when she was home alone. The kids were at school and her husband was gone. Due to Michelle's injuries, she spent a lot of time resting in one of the comfortable chairs in the living room. On this particular day, she decided to sit down and rest. It was late morning, and she immediately fell into a deep sleep. She was sleeping soundly when she was startled awake by a female voice crying, "Get up! Get up! Get up!" Michelle's eyes flew open. She looked at the clock and was surprised to see that six hours had passed since she sat down. That's not the strange part of this story; it was what Michelle saw next that makes it more interesting.

As she turned away from the clock, she saw the ghost of a woman standing in the archway between the living room and the foyer. The woman had long, straight hair that was either black or very dark brown. She wore straight bangs across her forehead. Michelle remembers her eyes the most. They were sunken and sad. The woman's facial expression was very somber. Michelle said she felt intense sympathy for the sad-looking ghost. She watched the apparition until it slowly faded away.

This female spirit visited numerous times after that. She appeared to be trying to be helpful. Michelle said early on, she made it clear to the spirit that if she were to live with the family, she would need to help out. Several times, Michelle would be sleeping when she heard the woman calling out to her to wake up. When that happened, it usually meant that something was wrong in the house. Michelle would get up and find one of her kids needed her, or the dogs needed to be let out, or a light may have been left on. For reasons like this, at times it was helpful having the ghost around, but that doesn't mean the family always felt comfortable around all the spirits in the house.

Liv, who was eleven years old at this time, had a room with a lot of paranormal activity. It was a beautiful bedroom that was perfect for a young lady. The room boasted a nice bed, a beautiful dresser and was about fourteen feet by twelve feet. As attractive as this room was, Liv was terrified of it. She talked about a little girl who would pull the sheets off her bed while she was sleeping. Although Liv was used to that kind of activity happening in their Nebraska house, it seemed a tad more sinister in this house. She insisted on sleeping with a night light, and still uses a night light to this day. Most nights would find her sleeping on the floor in her brother's bedroom. Her brother never said he experienced anything unusual at any of the family's homes. Although Liv and Michelle don't believe that for a second, it did make Liv feel safer that he hadn't reported anything strange happening in his room.

In 2011, Liv could no longer stand sleeping in her bedroom. There was another room that was being used for storage, and she decided to move into it. It was much smaller than her old room -- only nine feet by ten feet -- but Liv didn't care. She moved into the former storage room and her old bedroom became a game room.

The family's dogs didn't like the game room. They would sit outside and stare into it. The only way they would go into the room was if a family member was in there with them. Otherwise, they would never cross the threshold. Michelle could tell that they were scared by something, but she couldn't figure out what it was.

Michelle may have finally witnessed what the two dogs were seeing one day. She was walking down the hallway that led past the game room door. As she got in front of the doorway, something caused her to turn and look in the room. Standing motionless in front of the window was a dark figure. It had a shadowy appearance and its face was featureless. Despite its lack of eyes, Michelle felt the thing was watching her. She was unable to tell for certain if it was a man or a woman, but somehow she felt it was female. It caught her off guard, but she knew the house was haunted, so she just acknowledged the spirit and continued on down the hall.

One afternoon, Michelle heard something crash in her bedroom. When she went to investigate, she found a picture frame lying shattered on the floor. The wall that this picture was hanging from was about four feet from where the picture was now resting. Either the spirit was trying to get the family's attention, or it wasn't very fond of the type of flowers that were in the picture.

Later that evening, a nasty thunderstorm blew through the area. As usual when there was a

134

thunderstorm, Liv took refuge in bed with Michelle. At one point, Liv, who was snuggling behind her mom, looked into a mirror that was attached to the dresser. In the reflection, she saw a woman walk along the foot of the bed. The woman had long, dark hair and was wearing a white dress with a full skirt. The woman turned and started to walk along the side of the bed directly behind Liv. That was too much for Liv, who closed her eyes in fear. When she opened them, the woman was gone.

Out-of-place smells are another thing that the family encountered in the house on the cul-de-sac. They would smell something in the living room that Michelle described as, "a granny, White Shoulders, pungent kind of smell." She meant it was a very strong scent of the kind of perfume that a grandma would wear. They most frequently experienced this smell around an antique hutch that they bought in 2009. Of course when I heard this, a red flag went up. I wondered if there was a spirit attached to the antique hutch. They had lived there less than a year at that point, and odd things had been happening in the house almost from the beginning. Maybe the "grandma" spirit that came with the hutch was just the newest member of the ghostly brigade.   Another smell they noticed periodically was that of cigarette smoke, despite the fact that no one in the family smokes. You could argue that since smoke tends to soak into things, maybe a previous occupant had been a smoker and the smell had lingered. The strange thing was that the smoke odor would come and go, just as the perfume scent did. One moment it would be strong, and the next there would be no trace of it.

Another thing that Michelle mentioned about her family's time in the house on the cul-de-sac was that they started experiencing drastic mood swings. They would be happy one moment and sad the next. I believe the sad-looking entity that Michelle had seen in the living room was the cause of this phenomenon. It was if the people who lived there were affected by the ghost's sorrow.

A less disturbing, but certainly annoying thing that one of the ghosts did was to play with the trash can lid.

The trash can was the kind with a lid that swings back and forth. You push down on the front to deposit the trash, and then it swings back into position once you're done. Only with this trash can, the lid would move back and forth on its own. After a while, they just removed the lid completely.

Strange things also happened outside the house. There was a playground nearby that had a swing set. Sometimes, people walking on the paths or watching the children playing would see one of the swings start to move on its own. This would happen even on days when there was no wind. Only one of the two swings would move by itself. It was always the swing on the right, never the one on the left. If it were caused by wind, both swings would move. I don't think wind can be that selective.

One day, when Michelle was walking one of her dogs near the park, she paused to take photos of the hundreds of spider webs that were lying on top of the grass. Michelle noticed her dog begin to act strangely. It appeared to be following something through the grass. Michelle kept snapping photos, and in a couple of them, it appears that a misty form is trying to take shape.

Now, let's get into some of the neighbors' experiences. A woman named Heather lived in the house to Michelle's left. Heather's family also experienced a lot of paranormal activity during their time in the home. Heather's daughter began to have severe night terrors for the first time. She had always slept peacefully before, but something in this house seemed to cause her to wake up screaming in the middle of the night.

Lights were turned on and off when nobody was home. Doors would open and close, as well.

One night, when Heather's family was gone for the evening, Michelle was doing something in Liv's bedroom. If you looked through the bedroom window, you could see Heather's house. When Michelle glanced out the window, she saw a silhouette of a man standing in one of Heather's windows. The man was standing just far enough back from the glass that he was out of the light. It was too dark for Michelle to make out his features. If he would have taken a step forward, she said she was sure she could tell who he was. Unfortunately, not only did he not take that step forward, he decided to vanish right before her eyes.

Heather threw a "girls only" party one evening. All the women from the cul-de-sac were sitting in lawn chairs, having a wonderful time talking and laughing. All of a sudden, a wine glass that was sitting on a table tipped and spilled all over the table and patio. The women laughed it off. The glass was refilled the glass and they all started talking again. Moments later, another wine glass fell over. Nobody was near it at the time. Once the second glass fell, everyone avoided that table for the rest of the evening.

One of the women joked that it must be the spirit telling them to stop drinking. As that, the porch light came on. When Heather got up to check, she found that the light switch was in the "off" position. As she stood there, trying to figure out how the light had managed to come on without the switch being flipped, the light turned itself off.

Michelle suspected that a ghost had turned on the light in order to get their attention. She asked the spirit to turn the light back on. The light came on. This happened three to four times. Someone in the group snapped a photo and got a picture of a potential orb. Although I am skeptical of orbs, and it *is* an outdoor photo, which means the "orb" could be an insect or a dust particle, I did want to include it. None of the other photos taken that night contained anything that remotely resembled it.

Carissa lived in the house to the right of Michelle's. Her house had unexplained activity, as well. Carissa's experiences were a bit different than those that took place in the other two houses on the cul-de-sac. That could be because her house had a more playful spirit visiting it.

The first time she encountered the spirit, Carissa was in the kitchen and her three children were all upstairs playing. In the middle of the kitchen was an island. Carissa was working at the counter with her back turned

137

to the island. When she turned around, she saw a little boy who looked to be five or six years old standing near the island. He had brown hair that was cut in a bowl shape. He wore a white t-shirt and jeans and he looked very real to Carissa, so real that she thought he must be one of the neighborhood kids. She watched him for about five seconds before making her way toward him to see if he needed help. As she started to move, the boy was mysteriously gone. She didn't see him fade from view or run out of the room; he was just there one moment and gone the next. When she told her husband about it, he said that he had seen the same thing in the house several times. Usually when he saw the boy, he would be peeking around the corner. Carissa saw the boy several more times, but never as clearly as she did that day.

With their spirit being that of a child, you have to assume that there would be some playful activity as well. The family heard whispers on their baby monitor. Toys would find their way out of the toy box after they had just been put away. They would hear the sound of coins falling to the floor, but upon inspection, no coins would be found. Items would disappear and then reappear later. One time, they found the household scissors out in the yard.

One of my favorite things that happened to them involved the bathroom mirror. One morning Carissa was taking a shower and she neglected to turn the fan on. When she got out of the shower, the mirror was fogged up from the steam. Written in the steam were the words "Hi Cinnamon." Her husband wasn't there at the time, and although it could have been done the night before, he was adamant about not having done it. He said that if he had decided to play a prank by writing something on the mirror, he would have written "Boo" or something like that. Carissa had no idea who Cinnamon was.

I've always found mirror messages frightening. It all goes back to the movie *The Shining* with its lovely "redrum" message. I even had my own experience with a mirror message once. My wife and I were in Chicago this past January and we were staying in a hotel. I was in the shower, and when I got out, the words "Hey Sexy" were written on the mirror. When I saw that, I felt all special and good about myself. I haven't been feeling sexy in years so a message like that was special. After doing some sexy muscle flexing in the mirror, I made my way to the bedroom where my wife was and thanked her for the message. Well, she had no clue what I was talking about. She assured me she didn't leave the message. Needless to say, I didn't feel so sexy after that and my ego took a direct hit. I don't think it was anything ghostly. I am assuming it was written by someone who had that room before us.

Michelle mentioned that periodically, she would see lights coming on and off in Carissa's house when nobody was home. The strange thing about the paranormal activity in the houses on the cul-de-sac was that when one home was experiencing activity, the others were not. It's almost like the spirit would move from house to house. But it also seems like there may have been three different spirits present. There was the little boy that Carissa and her husband saw. Then there's the spirit that appeared to be a man in the window of Heather's house. In Michelle's house we have the ghost of a very sad woman.

If Hollywood got hold of this story, I am sure there are a lot of different angles they could take on what caused this activity. You have the hutch that could have a spirit attached to it. You have a male apparition and a sad female spirit. Maybe the male spirit is abusive and won't let the female move on. Maybe the boy at Carissa's house was the son of the female spirit, and she's sad because he is not with her. I don't really know what the cause of the hauntings was. In Michelle's case, they wanted the female spirit to come with them when they moved out of Scott Air Force Base and into their new home in Mascoutah. They did tell her she could come with them if she wanted, but as of yet, they have had no experiences at their new home. It seems that after almost twenty years of paranormal activity in her various homes, Michelle may have finally outrun it.

CLOSING

I hope you enjoyed the stories! I had fun gathering them. I wish I could have had the opportunity to investigate all the locations mentioned in this book, but due to other obligations, as well as the homeowner's privacy, it's not always feasible to conduct an investigation. I tried to tell the stories as best I could to make you feel like they were coming directly to you from the person who experienced them. I try and stay true to the facts of the stories as they were related to me.

If there's another book in the future for me, I hope that it will be full of more of my personal accounts. I am going to do my best to have some more adventures so that I can share them with you in a comedic and downright frightening way. Until then, if you haven't read my first book, please do. If you have read my first book, I thank you from the bottom of my heart. Even more, I thank you for giving me another chance to redeem myself with this book.

'Til next time, Happy Hauntings!

About the Author

Luke Naliborski is the investigations coordinator for the American Ghost Society, a paranormal speaker and writer as well as a tour guide for the Alton Hauntings ghost tours in Alton, Illinois. Luke has an uncanny way of delivering his stories in a manner that makes you think he's having a one-on-one conversation with you. Just you, Luke, and a blazing campfire to keep you company as he spins his web of ghostly tales. You'll laugh one second, learn the next, and wet yourself when you least expect it. Luke currently resides in Mascoutah, Illinois, with his beautiful wife Heather, daughter Iris, and son Jett. If you enjoyed this book, be sure to read his first book titled *The Lighter Side of Darkness*. As he says, "It's got thrills, it's got chills, it's got laughs, it's got romance!" Luke has also contributed stories to *So There I Was* and *Illinois Hauntings* by Troy Taylor.

WHITECHAPEL PRESS

Whitechapel Productions Press is a division of Apartment #42 Productions and a small press publisher, specializing in print and electronic books about ghosts and hauntings. Since 1993, the company has been one of America's leading publishers of supernatural books and has produced such best-selling titles as *Haunted Illinois, The Ghost Hunter's Guidebook, Ghosts on Film, Confessions of a Ghost Hunter, The Haunting of America, Sex & the Supernatural,* the *Dead Men Do Tell Tales* crime series and many others.

With more than a dozen different authors producing high quality books on all aspects of ghosts, hauntings and the paranormal, Whitechapel Press has made its mark with America's ghost enthusiasts.

You can visit Whitechapel Productions Press online and browse through our selection of ghostly titles, plus get information on ghosts and hauntings, haunted history, spirit photographs, information on ghost hunting and much more by visiting the internet website at:

WWW.WHITECHAPELPRESS.COM

Troy Taylor's
HISTORY & HAUNTINGS TOURS
Illinois
AND
American Hauntings

Find out more about tours, and make reservations online, by visiting the internet website at:

WWW.AMERICAN HAUNTINGS.ORG

Tours from American Hauntings include ghost tours in Illinois – including Alton, Chicago, Decatur & Lebanon – and the American Hauntings Tours that travel to haunted places and cities across the Country!

www.ingramcontent.com/pod-product-compliance
Lightning Source LLC
LaVergne TN
LVHW051642080426

835511LV00016B/2438